BENCHMARKING CUSTOMER SERVICE

GLEN PETERS

Pitman Publishing
128 Long Acre, London WC2E 9AN

A division of Pearson Professional Limited

First published in 1994

British Library Cataloguing in Publication Data
A CIP catalogue record for this book can be obtained from the British Library.

ISBN 0 273 61069 4

10 9 8 7 6 5 4 3 2

Phototypeset in Times Roman
Typeset by PanTek Arts, Maidstone, Kent
Printed and bound in Great Britain by
Biddles Ltd, Guildford and King's Lynn

The Publishers' policy is to use paper manufactured from sustainable forests.

CONTENTS

Acknowledgements vi

Introduction: From Arrogance to Passion vii

1 The Challenge of Change 1

2 Benchmarking at the Strategic Level 29

3 Benchmarking at the Process Level 73

4 Measurement and Analysis 111

5 Benchmarking to Enhance Shareholder Value 147

6 Case Studies in Benchmarking 173

Appendix I: A Benchmarking Project Plan 187

Appendix II: Example of Statistical Benchmarking Survey 203

Bibliography 211

Index 213

ACKNOWLEDGEMENTS

Much of this book would not have been possible without the hard work and creativity of my benchmarking team at Price Waterhouse who have laboured hard to help launch the Customer Excellence project throughout 1994. In particular Mike Crosswell, Philip Hendrick and Efrot Weiss. Mike Maskall, probably the most dynamic tax adviser I know, introduced me to the concepts of shareholder value discussed in this book and Frank Wetzel from New Jersey, the world's most unusual shrink, helped me develop the concepts of parallel learning and benchmarking competencies.

Patrick Beresford, our graphics wizard, has put up with the most ambiguous briefings from myself and produced illustrations which I hope will enhance your understanding of some of the concepts included. David Griffiths of Interactive Communications has provided me with some useful ideas for linking the topics in this book.

Last, but by no means least, many thanks to all my clients without whose support none of this would have been possible.

Glen Peters
July 1994

INTRODUCTION: FROM ARROGANCE TO PASSION

I believe that the biggest challenge facing companies is recreating the cult of the customer which Taylorism and megacorporations killed off at the turn of the century. This book is dedicated to those who have fought to bring back their organisations from the brink of disaster by re-engineering the customer back into their business and by creating an environment for employees to feel real passion for excellence in serving customers.

One of the most powerful ways of transforming our organisations is to observe how our most admired enterprises act and behave; the way they treat their customers and employees, and the unstinting belief that understanding customers and meeting their needs leads to long-term sustained profitability. This book is aimed at helping you to go about that process of observation and review, or in other words **benchmarking**.

In chapter 1 we set the scene for why we need to get smarter at retaining customers. I have also dedicated some discussion to what is customer service. Many people have a rather narrow definition of the term and we need to look at the life cycle of the customer–supplier relationship to begin to understand the enormous scope of customer service. We then define benchmarking within the context of customer service and how it might be applied to our organisations at a number of different levels.

In chapter 2 we borrow a model from the world of anthropology to discuss how tribal cultures map on to organisations and how you might assess where you are with regard to the three customer-orientated cultures of *arrogance, complacence* and *passion*. We also take a look at the competencies organisations need to serve customers and the professions from which they could benchmark these competencies – a technique we have developed called **Parallel learning**.

Chapter 3 plunges into the meat of benchmarking customer processes and is based on work which my team at Price Waterhouse has been conducting over 1993–94. The framework for benchmarking customer processes is adapted from the Malcolm Baldridge and European Quality Award criteria and should be topical for anyone involved in the management of organisational change. Most of the chapter follows a case study which we use for training our own benchmarking assessors.

In chapter 4 we look at some of the techniques of measurement and analysis such as focus groups and mystery shopper programmes. I believe that it is important to relate customer satisfaction as measured by these techniques to similar products and services on offer by other enterprises. What customers feel about your offer must be gauged in relation to what other choices your customers perceive they have. Hopefully this chapter will prompt you to incorporate more benchmarking data into your future surveys.

In chapter 5 we look at the measurement of change. What do we do with the benchmarking output? How do we manage the change? I have included a short discussion on shareholder value because there are still a few senior managers who remain to be convinced that a focus on customer driven change is good for the long-term viability of the business. The topicality of shareholder value today also justifies a connection between excellence in customer service and enhancing the equity of the owners of the enterprise.

Finally, in chapter 6 we include a case study of our own benchmarking project on customer processes. This is partly intended as an advertisement, should you wish to join, and as an aid for you to plan your own benchmarking venture. In Appendix I we provide you with a task plan for a benchmarking project in your own organisation. In Appendix II you will find an example of a benchmarking questionnaire.

All of the examples in this book are in the public domain and none of the views expressed of any organisation or individual are necessarily those of Price Waterhouse.

I hope this book helps you to stimulate enough good ideas for improving customer management in your organisation, but perhaps most importantly we hope it helps you evaluate your own enterprise's position in the journey towards customer passion.

1

THE CHALLENGE OF CHANGE

During a recent trip to the Far East I checked into Hong Kong's Mandarin hotel after a tiring ten-hour flight from Melbourne. Switching on the television to catch the CNN news I happened to get Channel 1, the in-house information channel.

'Every morning', the programme began, 'the management of this hotel meet to discuss one topic, their guests'. I sat on the edge of my bed to listen to the rest of the commercial which went on to exude an obsession with ensuring that guests who stayed at the hotel were being looked after to their satisfaction.

Like many of the Mandarin's past customers, I shall definitely go back there again because what stuck in my mind about the powerful message in the video was the talk about customers; in contrast, in most of the organisations whose management meetings I attend have an absolute paucity of talk about customers.

WATCH OUT FOR ENDLESS HOURS OF TALK

Take a note at your next monthly executive meeting and add up the endless hours of talk about the 'figures for the month ending...' or the new company strategy being promulgated by the new man at the top, or the office move, or the tenth re-organisation this year, or the implementation problems with yet another computer system for the finance department, or yet another product launch in Cannes, car parking, attendance, secretarial problems, the phone and so on. All sound familiar?

Yet at the Mandarin Hotel they seem to have got into the habit of talking everyday about customers. Just think of the benefits that will bring. Like over 95 per cent of their customers, I will keep coming back and because that is so obviously good for business, the 'figures' and a lot of all that other 'bureaucratic stuff' will almost take care of themselves.

There is an organisation where the management team are in constant contact with the needs of their customers and as a consequence are able to make decisions in the full knowledge of what it might mean for customers.

Let's contrast that with my bank where I've been a customer at one of their City branches for just over twenty years. I would imagine that my account has been a most profitable one, yet to the bank I'm just a 7-digit number with a sort code. The only time I ever hear from them is when they want to sell me something, tell me off or just tell me something *fait accompli.*

Recently, for example, they shut down my branch, sacked the manager and moved my account to another branch, and I'm sure the whole exercise can be wholly justified as a necessary cost reduction initiative. But at no time was I consulted or my views sought over any likely disruption, inconvenience or loss of relationship that might occur. And I'd bet that no other customers were either.

WHO LISTENS TO CUSTOMERS?

I can count on the fingers of one hand the number of times the views of customers have been sought with regard to repositioning or strategic study of a company. It's painful to have to admit it, but customers are often regarded as an afterthought. Their presence is felt vaguely in the background and of course they will always be there won't they? When organisations engage in take overs, mergers, joint ventures and so on, they make a number of risky assumptions about customers, the most dangerous of which is that they will keep coming back for more.

As business people faced with commercial reality, we go to great lengths to value our organisation's traditional assets such as plant, real estate and infrastructure. Yet perhaps the most valued asset, our customers, gets superficial treatment. The truth is that customers are more and more often voting with their feet and as they are offered a wider choice in products and services they abandon companies which offer poor or indifferent service in favour of others.

In the UK many of the privatised corporations lost more than half their market share within five years of deregulation in the business-to-business sector. And fewer than half 'The Times 1000' companies which existed ten years ago are no longer listed. Many management gurus believe that in the next ten years we will witness a rate of change significantly faster than what it has been over the last decade.

At a recent customer management forum of 200 companies, we established that 70 per cent of them stated customer retention was their number one priority. There were three reasons provided for this shift in emphasis towards customers:

- *Slow or near stagnant growth rates.* This will make new customers harder to find. Most predictions for growth over the next two years are in the region of around 2 per cent, so it is unlikely that we can look forward to a vast influx of customers seeking out products and services. Recovery will be slow, and there will continue to be fewer customers to replace the ones that leave us every year.
- *Increasing competition throughout Europe.* With President Clinton's powerful push on world trade, increased pressure on GATT agreements will see the entry of a number of highly service-orientated US companies into previously protected markets. Add to this further initiatives on privatisation, deregulation and EC trade agreements and any previous mantle of protection that had been afforded to existing markets will break away. Our customers will continue to have more choice and we will have to work harder to hold on to them.
- *Shareholder pressure.* Our shareholders will continue to put pressure on companies to return to the levels of profitability enjoyed in the 1980s, and to this many companies have responded by cutting overheads. For example, over the last four years BP Oil have halved their headcount in Europe. Now their splendid Britannic Towers HQ in Moorgate, built in the 1960s when oil companies oozed money, stands almost empty as thousands of employees no longer have jobs.

However, it is becoming obvious that there is increasing disillusionment in the reduction of overhead cost as the major tool for improving profitability and attention is now being directed towards customer retention as a superior strategy.

2% EXTRA CUSTOMER RETENTION = 10% OVERHEAD REDUCTION

In 1991, the management consultancy Bain made the claim that a 2 per cent improvement in customer retention would have the same profit impact as a 10 per cent reduction in overheads (Figure 1.1). If we consider the amount of pain, hardship and difficulty which

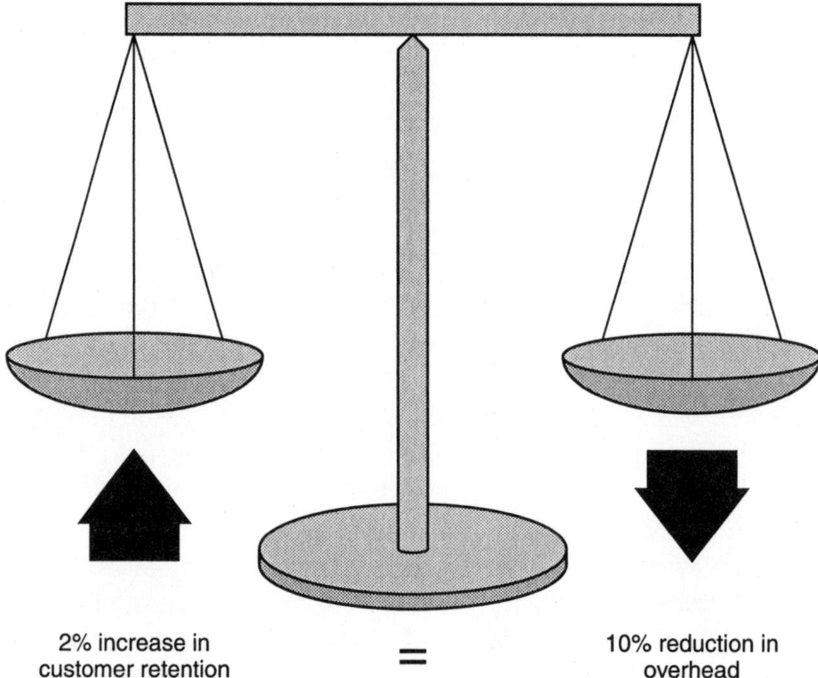

Figure 1.1 Bain's findings in the early 1990s reinforced earlier research by the Strategic Planning Institute that companies which focus on customer retention witness substantial increases in profitability. The statistic that on balance a 2% increase in retention has the same impact on profitability as a 10% decrease in overhead was widely publicised.

will be inevitable in achieving the 10 per cent reduction, then customer retention soon appears a more positive and sustainable means of achieving profit improvement.

Despite the obvious benefits from customer retention, many companies still continue to make deep cuts in their headcount and overheads to the point where they may now have seriously undermined their ability to service their existing customers. For many of these companies customer retention may now be the only choice left for survival.

The economics of customer retention can be stated in this simple arithmetic progression:

- Assume that every day one customer who normally spends between £50 and £100 each week stops buying in favour of a competitor.
- In the following year this equates to the lost sales of between £1 million and £2 million.
- If ten customers were to defect each day then the loss equates to between £10 and £20 million in the following year.

Many organisations report retention rates of around 80 per cent, which means that from a base of, say, a million customers just under 550 would be defecting every day. Since it is generally considered that the cost of acquiring a new customer to replace the one that has left can be up to 10 times the cost of maintaining an existing customer, the acquisition costs will result in a massive reduction in profitability (Figure 1.2).

So although it is clear that an increase of a few percentage points in customer retention should have a dramatic improvement in profitability, year after year we appear to observe with nonchalance this lemming-like behaviour. Just how long can we ignore the damaging consequences of thousands of our customers leaving our organisations never to return?

It must be said that customers generally choose to defect elsewhere only because they are no longer satisfied with the service they are being provided with. Yet, amazingly, almost 80 per cent of the organisations researched do not link reward to the sales force or other frontline teams with customer satisfaction.

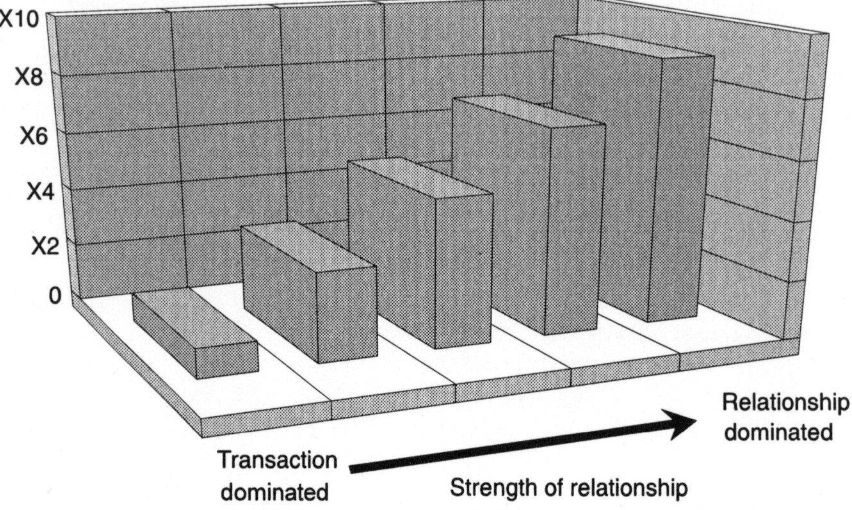

Figure 1.2 The cost of acquiring new customers varies with the commercial arrangement between customer and supplier. Where there is a strong and personal relationship behind each transaction (as in the case of consultancy for example) the cost will be at its highest. In contrast, where the transaction is simpler and involves less of a personal relationship (as in mail order shopping perhaps) the cost will be lower.

Furthermore few of the top management visit customers to discover at first hand their difficulties and frustrations in doing business with their organisations. In short, very few companies incorporate a measurement of customer satisfaction as a key management tool. The customer satisfaction director of Northern Telecom has this to say on the subject: 'The only assurance that customers will stay loyal today is if they're delighted, not merely satisfied'.

Keeping the customer satisfied does not only reduce the likelihood of defection, it also significantly increases the chance of gaining new customers through recommendation. We can see from Figure 1.3 that in the automotive sector only the highest levels of customer satisfaction will lead to a recommendation.

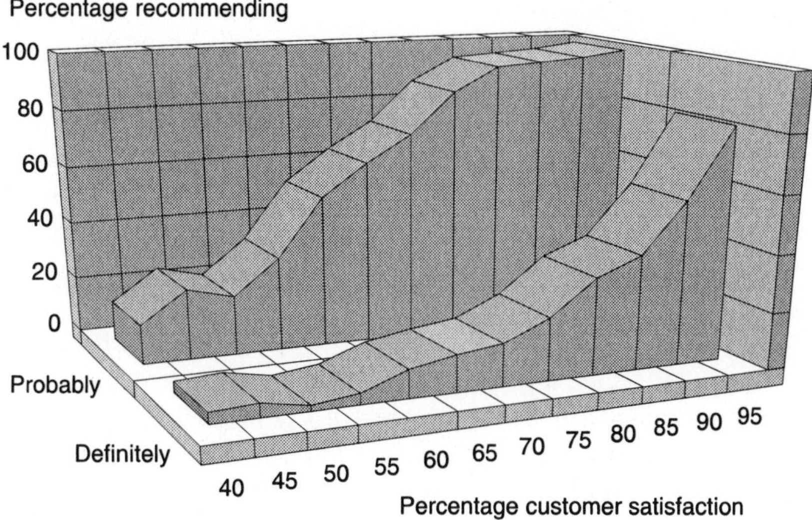

Figure 1.3 Research shows that customers who would definitely recommend a product or service to others need to be delighted rather than merely satisfied. This analysis from the automotive sector shows that far more respondents will 'probably' recommend purchases with average satisfaction results. Relatively few will 'definitely' recommend with a significant number only doing so at satisfaction percentages above 85-90%.

But making customers delighted doesn't come easy, especially for organisations which have enjoyed a protected or monopoly status, or for those which have been buoyed by historical events such as innovative products and long-term patent protection. Sadly, all good things come to an end, and as Thomas Kuhn, the man who coined the cliche 'Paradigm shift', suggested, success can become an organisation's worst enemy.

There is no doubt that retaining customers starts with excellence in customer service, and this is the subject we must now consider.

THE CHALLENGE OF CHANGE

I have called this chapter '*The Challenge of Change*' because I believe that the biggest challenge facing companies in the mature, slow-growth markets of OECD economies is to change their culture to one that is more focused on the customer.

Competition has increased with the advent of GATT, the introduction of deregulation and many other initiatives for change. Customers now have more and more choice so it is clear that we have to work that much harder at keeping them loyal to our organisations. We have to cast off the baggage of nearly a century of Taylorism – the management–union divide and megacorporations which have sought to distance employees from their customers.

To do this we will need to learn from organisations which have already embarked on this long journey back to the heart of the customer. Companies like Xerox, which began the process ten years ago and came back from near extinction; like Rover, which has transformed itself from a Soviet-like image to one of Europe's most successful companies; like ICL, the Information Technology company, which has come from being the vendor that everybody most wanted to ditch to one with probably the most loyal customer following and the most profitable in Europe.

We will also need to learn from organisations which have resisted the habit of de-personalising the customer into an amorphous mass called *the market*. We must learn from the small businesses where everybody meets the customer and they know their livelihood depends on them; and the village store, where perhaps the most advanced model for customer intimacy exists; and retailers such as Stewart Leonard, the controversial US entrepreneur who has imbued a culture which listens to the voice of the customer.

Marketing departments are today in crisis. A McKinsey report recently criticised marketing departments as being out of touch with their customers and often dwelling on irrelevant brand messages. These same departments are guilty of masquerading price discounting as special promotions and frequently they are seen more as a millstone around an organisation's neck.

Fewer than 25 per cent of marketing departments have responsibility for customer service and as little as a third are involved in total quality programmes. Is it not possible that the marketing director runs the risk of becoming extinct?

We must not forget historical models. For example, the artisans of the seventeenth-century renaissance who needed to be highly customer responsive to their sponsors. Their livelihoods depended on a sponsor who was satisfied with their artistic output and what he received in return for his philanthropy.

Benchmarking is going to become an important lever for change. Seeing how other people do it is far easier than inventing it yourself. Indeed, the Japanese have built their economy on this concept, a principle they call *Zenbara*.

Why don't we do the same? We seem reluctant to engage in this legalised form of copying because perhaps our early education has discouraged plagiarism and encouraged creativity and self-help. In some instances we are arrogant enough to believe that our organisations possess unique characteristics which put them on a pedestal above all others.

WHAT EXACTLY IS CUSTOMER SERVICE?

Most people's definition of customer service is a narrow one. It arises from the way companies have themselves relegated the concept of service to an activity which is perceived to add little value. Picture the signs which say 'Parts and Service' in most garages and it conjures up an image of grimy counters attended by disgruntled grimy personnel, servicing grimy weekend DIY motorists. Or the endless queues at the customer services desk of your retail department store.

At a survey we conducted recently of 200 companies we found that managers believe the position of service in the overall offer will increase in relation to the core product. Figure 1.4 shows how three years ago 50 per cent of managers believed that the core product was all important in delivering satisfaction, while three years from now 45 per cent of them believe service will be the key differentiation in the mix between branding product and services. If it is going to be the case that service will be so important in winning and retaining customers then we need to work hard to promote its image to customers and to take a broad view of how service delivers value to the customer.

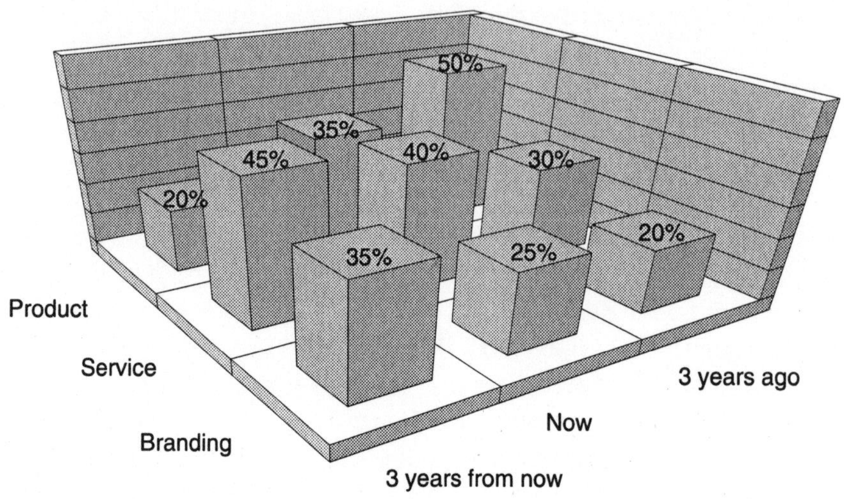

Figure 1.4 We polled opinions from a collection of managers representing customer facing activities on the importance of the three components of an organisation's offer: the branding, the service proposition and the core product. The results indicated that their perception of the relative issue of the three components would change in favour of customer service within the next three years.

Figure 1.5 illustrates how service delivers value, and it is based on work by Dr Milind Lele from the University of Marketing Management in Chicago. Customer value from a product or service can occur in any of three stages:

- the purchase;
- while in use;
- in disposal.

Organisations need to understand where in the three stages their products add the greatest value. For example, in certain areas of retailing it is known that customers 'love to shop'. They get their greatest value in the pursuit of the purchase. So in this case, retailers have to concentrate their service offer in areas such as the quality and proficiency of the sales channels, in the packaging and presentation of goods, helpful and friendly staff who make the customer feel good and ease of payment method.

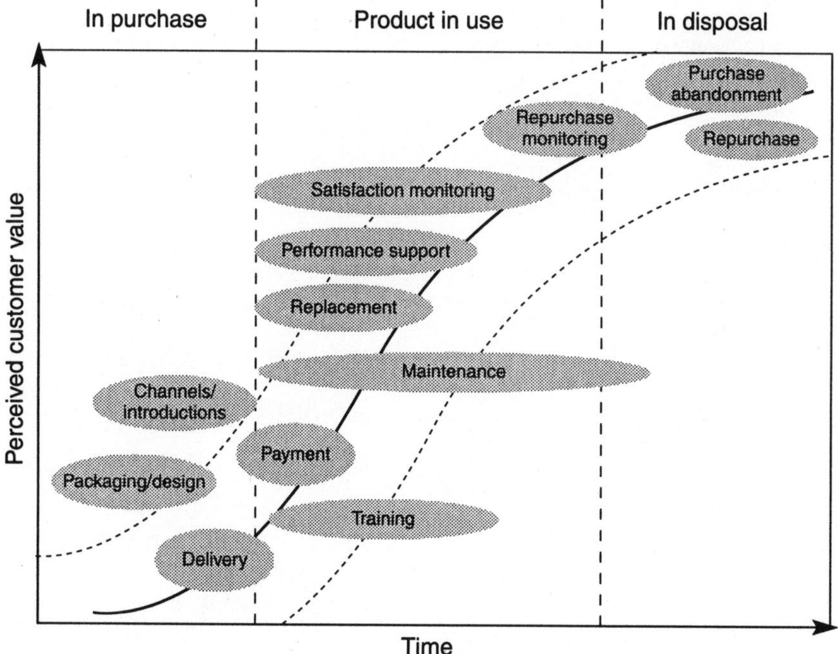

Figure 1.5 The curves show the relationship of time to perceived value of customer service. Packaging, accessibility of sales channels and speed of delivery usually contribute to adding value at the 'purchase' stage of the life cycle. Quality of technical support, training, reliability of maintenance call outs, the ease of getting problems fixed and defective products replaced all add value for certain products while in use. At the disposal stage for certain products, assistance with replacement of new alternatives and monitoring repurchase intentions can ensure the customer will return to repurchase.

Clearly, if one is catering for a segment where customers 'love to shop' then herding them around like cattle and making it an unpleasant experience will not bring them back again.

The customer who goes shopping for a family car will probably be more interested in the service quality while the car is in use and in the residual value on 'trade in' options when he wishes to replace it in three years time. So to keep this sort of customer happy, the vendor must offer affordable and efficient maintenance, replacement guarantees if the car is a dud, a commitment to satisfaction

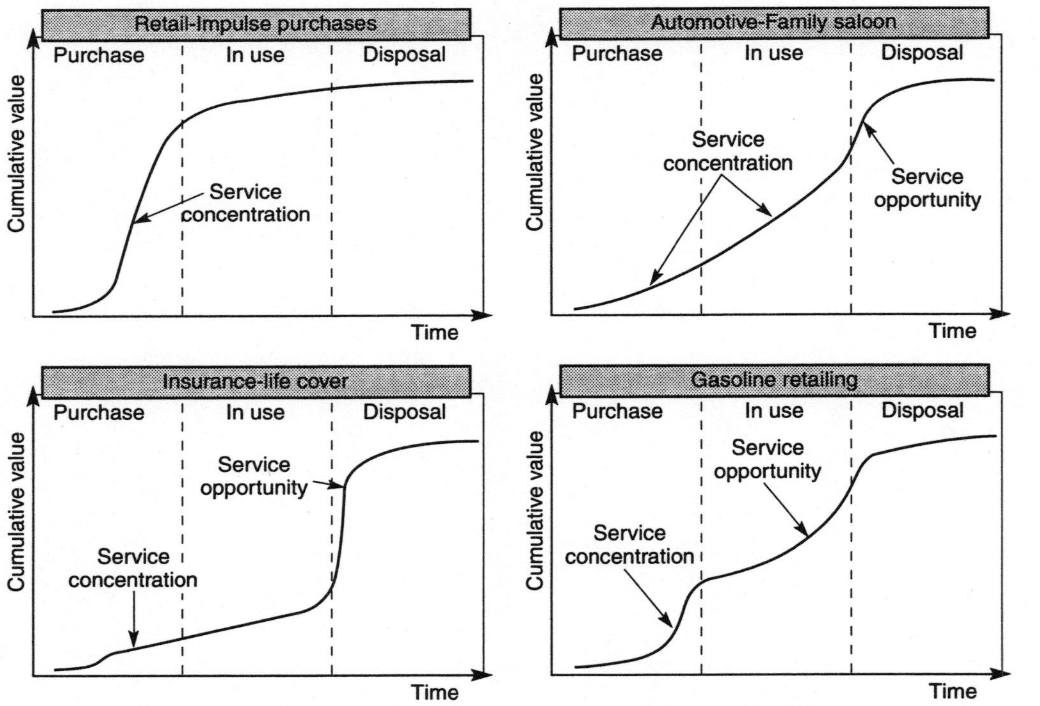

Figure 1.5(a) Here are some examples of how customers derive value from products and services at the three stages of purchase, use and disposal. Impulse retail purchases are usually concentrated at the purchase level. With long-term purchases such as the family saloon product value continues through purchase and use with an opportunity for additional service assistance at or near the disposal stage. Few automotive suppliers have got the knack of getting to their customers at this important stage. Similarly, with life insurance services nearly all the perceived value of the product comes at the disposal stage when policies mature. Few customers are given assistance at this critical point. In gasoline retailing the greatest value is on the use of the fuel yet few companies have been able to meet this need.

and trade in offers at the disposal stage to ensure they come back to purchase again.

In one of the fastest growing segments of the car market, Land Rover are one of a few automotive suppliers who offer specialist training for customers who purchase Range Rovers. Customers are taken for a 3–4 hour driving lesson on rutted soggy 50 per cent gradients to show off the performance of the 4-wheeled machines. Customers who buy a Discovery or Range Rover get a telephone call or questionnaire asking about the performance of their purchase. In one legendary story, a Land Rover security man on duty over Christmas was able to deal with a stranded driver in former Yugoslavia, arranging for spares to be dispatched and offering advice on fitting.

Life insurers must be aware that the value to customers of their life policy increases as maturity date approaches. Although most sales literature promotes the prospect of long-term security and middle-aged leisure when a policy matures, few insurers actually have an attractive service offering at this stage. Customers are given little guidance on the options on extending their policy or securing their cash payouts in alternative investments. There is an awful feeling that having paid the premiums over a period of years, the insurers become less and less interested in their customers.

In gasoline retailing, oil companies offer service at the time of purchase when the motorist gets only limited value. While filling up with fuel he may take the opportunity of washing the car or topping up the air in the tyres. The greatest value perceived is in use of the fuel and companies have missed a number of service opportunities during this stage. The motorists' top concern is whether he is getting the most value out of the fuel he purchases. Fuel consumption cards by type of vehicle would, for example, give motorists the opportunity of tracking their mileage and fuel consumption to indicate whether their vehicle was working at maximum efficiency. Closer links with the car manufacturers may also help to promote fuel management systems.

Figure 1.5a illustrates these purchasing examples.

Benchmarking is about improving competitive position and using *best practice* to stimulate radical innovation rather than seeking minor, incremental improvements on historic performance. Often I hear people comment that benchmarking is simply the process of measuring how well or otherwise a business is doing according to its plans, or in relation to its competition. I would see that as rather like saying that a slimming plan is all about weighing yourself from time to time.

In our view, benchmarking is about taking action, not collecting data and comparing it euphemistically or pessimistically. But to continue with the analogy I have started, you would not start a slimming plan without first deciding that you weigh too much, and then setting the goals you wish to reach.

BENCHMARKING

There's a joke going around the circuit in North America in the last year that goes along the following lines. 'What's the difference between a Lexus and a Mercedes?' You've probably guessed it – $30,000.

To many people in the automotive trade in North America and to a certain extent here in western Europe, the Lexus appears to be a copy of the Mercedes. All the Japanese appear to have done is to find a way of producing it and manufacturing it at a price that is significantly cheaper. This Japanese technique, *Zenbara*, could be described as legally stealing other people's products and ideas. It's not a new technique – it's been practised by the automotive industry since the 1930s, except then, and now, we call it value engineering and many cars we see today on the roads have been copied or 'Zenbara'd' or value-engineered some time in their design process. Many would also probably agree with the view that the Lexus is not just a lower-priced copy of the Mercedes but also a superior car. *Zenbara* not only seeks to copy best practice but also to improve the resulting product.

However, the copying of operational management practices has been relatively new. Perhaps the first recorded such incident was when Rank Xerox's patents for their world famous photocopiers expired towards the end of the 1970s. Japanese manufacture's like Canon were quick off the mark to introduce carbon copies in the lucrative North American market, and surprise surprise, at a price significantly cheaper than Xerox were able to achieve. Like the Lexus in the last two years has captured some 70 per cent of the market dominated by Mercedes, Canon photocopiers played havoc with Rank Xerox's market share in the 1980s.

Fortunately at the time, Rank Xerox had a Japanese subsidiary and they set about, through that subsidiary, trying to find out a way in which they could manufacture their own copiers at costs similar to their Japanese competitors.

So here we saw the North Americans using *Zenbara* in reverse, doing what the Japanese had been doing for years – 'why invent it when you can pinch it from others'. The Japanese got to the top of the manufacturing league by learning from the best through the 1950s and 1960s. Here was a North American company working out how to implement Japanese management practices in its own plants in North America to reduce its own manufacturing costs. The technique of benchmarking as it later began to be called, was promoted aggressively by Rank Xerox within the company and some time around 1985 they published a milestone paper in the *Harvard Business Review*.

So benchmarking is a process of learning from other organisations ways of improving your business. Most companies today practise benchmarking in one way or another. Very few practise benchmarking with the vigour and structured approach adopted by companies like Xerox. At Xerox requests for capital projects have to be accompanied by benchmarks and at Unilever new products are thoroughly benchmarked against competing offers before being launched.

In fact when you mention benchmarking to most managers they often say 'Ah, but of course we've been doing that for years'. Sure, they go for lunch to visit a colleague or contact in another company and talk about how company X is preparing itself for, say, the new social chapter, or how they tackle transfer pricing. At the moment there appears to be an endless pilgrimage of European managers off to visit US companies for a week or ten-day 'jolly'. I suspect that these attempts lead to very little action. From talking to colleagues it appears that many of these visits are unstructured, they take a lot of time to set up and frequently lead to information that is nice to have but hard to act upon.

It is my estimate that although benchmarking is practised by over 75 per cent of companies today, fewer that 10 per cent of companies have actually institutionalised benchmarking into their management practices.

Very few companies today in western Europe use benchmarks to design new service offerings, or as part of an on-going continuous improvement programme. Indeed, I would even go as far as saying that the majority of companies today in Europe do not even know their own benchmarks for such critical areas such as inventory, average lead times, defect rates and customer service levels. In a survey that we recently conducted it surprised us that less than 10 per cent of companies actually had reliable data on their own critical benchmarks.

But why should we benchmark? Is this another management fad? Surely today's manager has 1001 more important tasks to be getting on with?

Well, let's accept that continuous improvement within our business is going to be critical to survival. Wage rates are not going to fall in any marked way, and with the increase in and globalisation our competitors are going to come from areas and countries that we wouldn't have dreamed of only a few years ago. If we are going to make these dramatic improvements in our business we need all the ideas and the inspiration to cause a step-change in productivity, in efficiency and in the service levels we offer our customers. Benchmarking has got to be one of the quickest and most reliable ways of finding techniques and opportunities to emulate the brightest and the best in both our sectors and in other sectors which share similar problems.

The significant increase in popularity of benchmarking has also seen a significant shift in its emphasis. Whereas in the past it may have been the case to benchmark a product's physical and tangible features, such as cost and functionality, now it is more likely to concentrate on value and business processes.

It is no longer adequate to build a better mousetrap, because the world may not necessarily beat a path to your door just because of the quality of the product itself. This old adage has been replaced by the broader and more responsible view that improving the processes by which customers are gained and retained is more likely to build a better and longer-term business.

BENCHMARKING AS A PROCESS OF MANAGING CHANGE

Benchmarking should follow these four steps (Figure 1.6):

1. **Identify** – It is a continuous process which must be built into the company's culture and management processes. It cannot and must not be allowed to be a one-off exercise.
2. **Analyse** – The sole purpose is to identify areas for improvement and results should not be used either to provide a pat on the back ('We're doing okay – we are in the top three already') or as a stick to beat departments with ('Why aren't you lot as good?').
3. **Plan** – This aims to identify and state clearly 'best practice' in functions or processes, both inside and outside the organisation's business sector.
4. **Implement and evaluate** – This must lead to very specific action. As we have stated already, benchmarking is all about implementation and not about data collection.

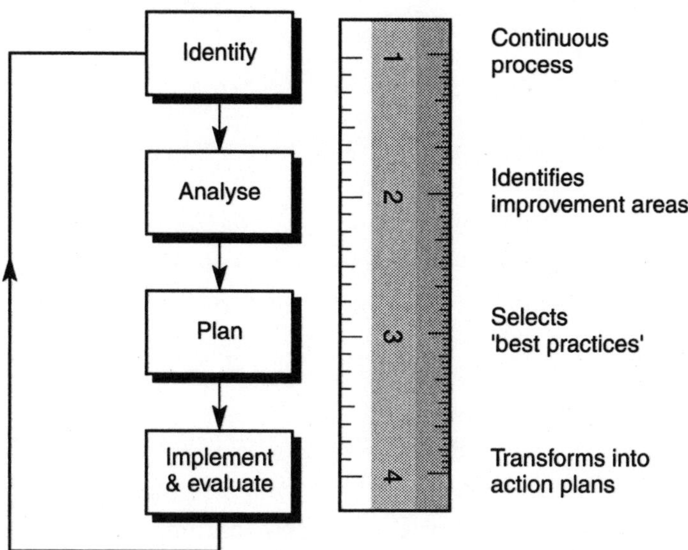

Figure 1.6 The four steps of the benchmarking process.

Later in chapter 5 we shall discuss how to go about implementation as part of a process of managing change.

A DEFINITION OF BENCHMARKING?

Benchmarking is about improving competitive position, and using best practice to stimulate radical innovation rather than just seeking minor, incremental improvements on historic performance.

WHY DO IT? MIGHT IT NOT STIR UP MORE MUDDY WATER THAN IT HOPES TO CLEAR?

Through benchmarking it is possible to gain five clear benefits.

1. Customer requirements can be more readily met.
2. Best practices will be brought into awareness and actively examined.
3. Goals will be established with an external perspective.
4. True measures of productivity and customer satisfaction can be established.
5. A more competitive position will be obtained.

Benchmarking seeks not to muddy the waters by stirring up the silt, but to cleanse it by a gradual and careful filtration process. In this analogy, the best practice is simple and unarguable – everyone knows that clean, clear, fully purified water is worth striving for.

SO WHO DO WE BENCHMARK AGAINST?

The first and most obvious organisations to benchmark against would be those operating in your own sector – your direct competitors. It's clear that in all aspects of sales, marketing the product and the general customer interface you need to be aware of your competitors' offerings and match or improve them where necessary.

Over 90 per cent of people today, for example, who go on a Club Mediterane holiday use the services of that organisation again. Many other holiday package companies will be pleased if even 10 or 20 per cent of their customers maintain that level of brand loyalty. Club Mediterane is doing something which the other holiday operators might like to emulate to improve their brand loyalty. Here is a clear opportunity for benchmarking.

But benchmarking is not just confined to companies within your own sector. Indeed, it makes it rather difficult to get hold of confidential data from your competitors. Clearly it's easier to share best practice benchmarking with non-competing companies. Many people who have done benchmarking in organisations outside their sector report that they have experienced great creative breakthroughs by doing so. Some maintain that the opportunities for business improvement within their sector are relatively few. The real creative leaps lie outside their sector.

It is reputed that South-West Airlines, for example, has improved the turnaround times for their planes – i.e., getting passengers off, cleaning the planes, servicing them and refuelling them. They have achieved this by benchmarking car maintenance crews at the Indianapolis rally. They studied how these crews managed to turn around the high-technology racing machines in seconds rather than hours.

In total contrast, Dominos Pizzas went to a hospital emergency ward to study how crews mobilised themselves in minutes to respond to a crisis. A telecommunications company, an airline and a home banking service have plenty in common, although none of these companies are strict competitors as such. The common bond is that they communicate and make sales with customers at the other end of the telephone and therefore valid benchmarks are possible.

THE THREE LEVELS OF BENCHMARKING

Benchmarking falls into three broad categories (Figure 1.7).

Strategic Benchmarking

Strategic benchmarking is at the level where we're able to compare and contrast the strategic mission and direction of the company – its culture, its people and the skills it employs in achieving this mission.

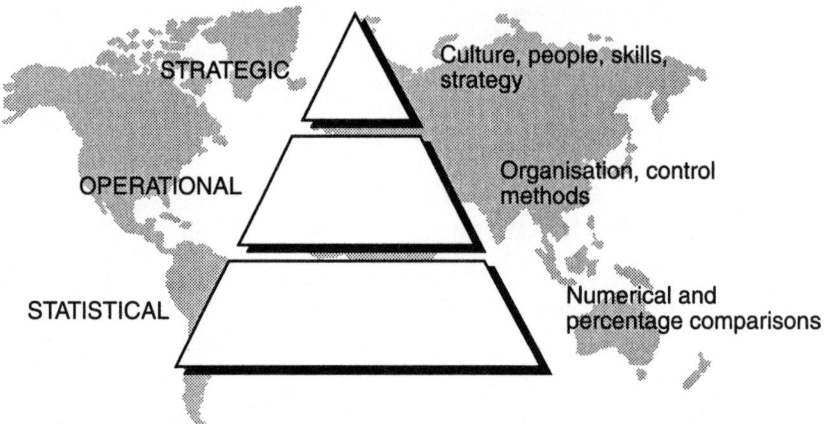

Figure 1.7 Benchmarking can be conducted at three levels: the strategic, the process and the statistical level. You need to use the appropriate level when drawing business conclusions.

If anyone has stayed, for example, at a Ritz Carlton Hotel, the plaque on the wall declares their mission to be 'Ladies and gentlemen serving ladies and gentlemen'. The mission appears clearly followed through in the way that you're greeted by the driver in the courtesy bus from the airport to the hotel all the way through to reception, hotel porters and the catering staff. This is an up-market offering based on traditional values.

However, stay at other hotel chains and you have a very confused offering. No clear indication of strategy, high variability in service levels from one city to another and in some cases a level of indifference from its staff.

General Electric have a simple plan called the 10/15 strategy, launched by General Electric's Chief Executive Officer, Jack Walsh. The company needs to turn its inventory ten times a year and realise a 15 per cent return on sales. A simple but powerful message.

Process benchmarking

Here we are looking at methods, procedures and the business processes of the organisation. How do they run their treasury, for example? How does Exxon publish an annual result within five working days from year end, whereas it takes other multinationals three weeks? How does Kawasaki, the Japanese manufacturer, manage to hold on average three days of inventory in its factories when the closest European competitor needs three weeks? Why have private parcel delivery services taken up to 90 per cent of market share from their state-owned counterparts? How does one mail order company manage to get products to customers within 24 hours, whereas its closest rival takes between a week and ten days?

It is at the process level where I believe we have the 'liquid gold', the 'real fire' in benchmarking.

Statistical benchmarking

Statistical benchmarking is about performance measures and is frequently the point at which people start. There are vast arrays of performance indicators, such as sales calls per man days, invoices per man year, rate of defects per unit of production, etc.

The numbers on their own are meaningless. Many companies today gather these statistics, sometimes at huge cost, but in isolation they provide relatively little information on which to act to improve the management of business processes. At an Amsterdam night club the statistic that 85 per cent of men are bald has a number of conclusions. Clearly a possible conclusion that watching women take their clothes off makes you go bald would be misleading.

For benchmarking to be effective we need to structure our research so that all three levels – the strategic, the process and the statistical level – all tie up.

INTERNAL BENCHMARKING

Many organisations have begun to use benchmarking as a mechanism for measuring the performance of their own internal functions or operating units without reference to measures outside the organisation. Many companies believe that internal benchmarking allows them greater access to information and helps under-performing units

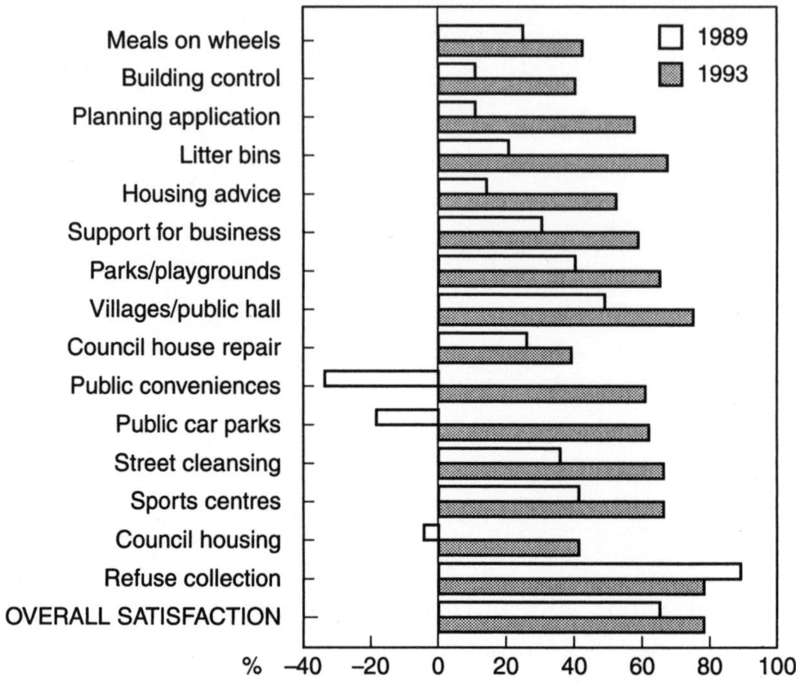

Figure 1.8 Internal benchmarking as practiced by Braintree District Council.

to aim for the best practice of their top-performing units. Figure 1.8 shows how Braintree District Council compares satisfaction scores for a number of their services.

USING THE THREE LEVELS OF BENCHMARKING FOR CUSTOMER SERVICE

Throughout this book we shall be seeing how the different levels of benchmarking can be applied to improving customer service. Figure 1.9 summarises the appropriateness of benchmarking to customer service. Generally, strategic benchmarks are useful in defining your service strategy and identifying the target culture required to deliver that strategy. Process benchmarks are more useful in initiating change in your organisation and statistical benchmarks help monitor the performance of your service offer.

	Reasons why we benchmark	Strategic benchmarking	Process benchmarking	Statistical benchmarking
1	Identifying a different business direction	✓		
2	Differentiating the service offering	✓	✓	✓
3	Indicators to initiate change		✓	
4	Changing the culture to one that is customer driven	✓		
5	Comparing the service offering		✓	✓
6	Monitoring operational service offerings			✓
7	Evaluating best practice		✓	
8	Use as a sales aid to demonstrate superior service			✓

Figure 1.9 The appropriateness of the three levels of benchmarking.

THE DIFFICULTIES OF BENCHMARKING CUSTOMER SERVICE

Customer service is the most intangible component of a product or service offer. Frequently its value is in its perception by customers and its delivery is entirely dependant on those people serving the customers. This presents difficulties for those who try to measure or institutionalise 'a passion for the customer'. In later chapters of this book we shall be exploring ways in which organisations can get around some of these difficulties by employing a range of qualitative and quantitative techniques.

Figure 1.10 Customer service benchmarking is often carried out looking at similar processes outside one's sector. Many organisations visit Disney to see how the passion for customer service is institutionalised in the day-to-day operations of the business.

Benchmarking can be very time consuming, and can provide many false starts, witness a project I initiated which has taken us between six and nine man months to set up. Choosing the right framework to carry out the measurement and its subsequent analysis requires some previous experience of having carried out this activity. Finally, I believe there is an art to producing actionable results. For example, if you choose far too high a goal or benchmark, say on a scale of 0 to 50, and you're trying to chase 40 when you are currently at a value of 5, you will probably find the objective unattainable and your action plans to get there meaningless. If you choose 20 as your target you might find that objective quite achievable.

In the subsequent pages of this book I offer you a number of tips and useful ideas to help you get the most out of benchmarking without going down too many blind alleys. The frameworks discussed are from my team's personal experiences of undertaking a pan-European customer service benchmarking exercise. I hope they are as helpful to you as they were to me.

On reading this chapter you should ask the following questions of your own enterprise:

1. Is customer retention a key strategy for your organisation?
2. Do you know how many customers leave every year?
3. Do you know how much potential revenue you loose from this attitude and how many customers you could keep loyal at little extra cost?
4. Do you know at which point from purchase to disposal, customer service adds the greatest value to customers?
5. Do you know which organisation you would most like to emulate? What do they do better than you?
6. Do you know your own benchmarks for the critical areas of customer service?
7. Do you have a customer service strategy?
8. Do you know how your strategy compares with the competition?
9. Did you do any benchmarking in evolving your service strategy?
10. Is benchmarking a regular management process in your organisation?

Results

- *Yes* to fewer than 3 questions should have you concerned about your future. You may not want to read the rest of this book.
- *Yes* to 3–6 questions and you have at least begun to appreciate the value of customer retention and how benchmarking may be able to help achieve that goal.
- *Yes* to more than 6 questions and you are in a minority of companies with a healthy attitude to customers and you appreciate the value of benchmarking. The rest of this book may only confirm your mission.

2

BENCHMARKING AT THE STRATEGIC LEVEL

In this chapter we discuss:

- How to benchmark service strategies.
- How to benchmark culture.
- How to benchmark skills and competencies.

At the strategic level, benchmarking is a three-phase process, developed from an understanding of the chosen organisation's customer mission. The first is to examine the chosen organisation's strategy towards customer service. The second is to appreciate how they involve their culture. The third is to learn how they exploit their skills and competencies.

BENCHMARKING SERVICE STRATEGY

Organisations usually choose one of the three service templates illustrated in Figure 2.1 as the basis of their strategy for delivering service excellence and thereby retaining their customers.

In selecting an organisation against which to benchmark you need to assess which strategic template it corresponds to and how it develops its vision, mission and philosophies to fit its service strategy.

1. Innovation

The first template concentrates on innovation and superior quality. Organisations adopt a 'get there first' strategy and accordingly need a service offering which guarantees technical excellence and the highest standards of quality. Into this category would fit Motorola (with their six sigma strategy) and 3M.

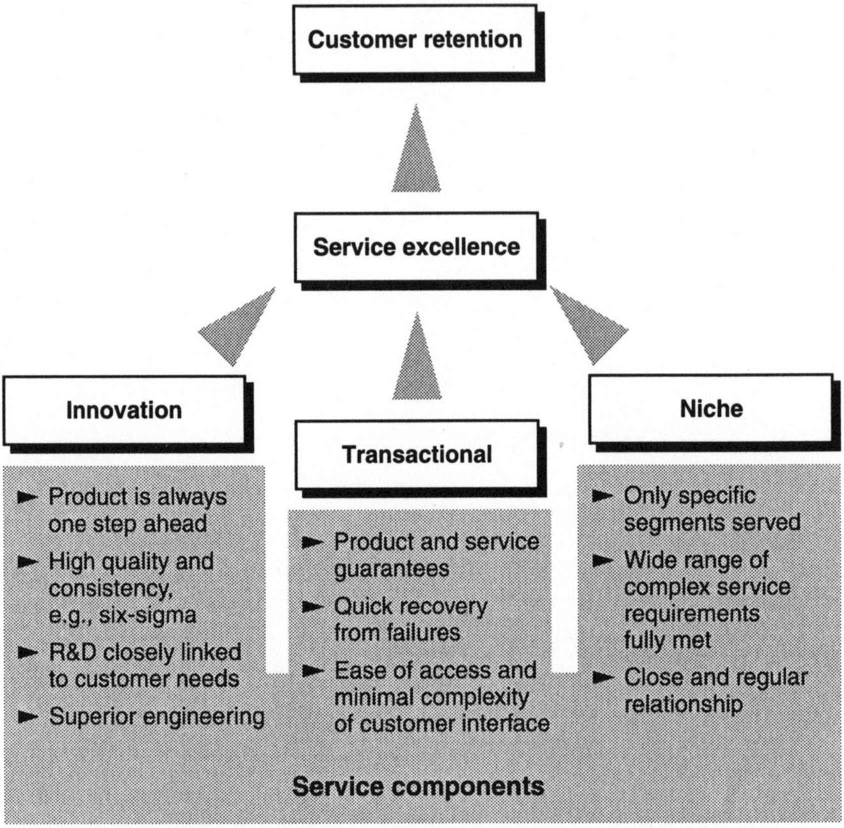

Figure 2.1 These are the three most commonly adopted templates of a service strategy. Each one has its own particular service components and these need to be developed the way customers see your offer. Innovative products must be based on superior engineering and extremely low failure rates. People do not want to be buying leading edge hi-fi for example which doesn't work when you bring it home. Transactional strategies must offer customers quick and easy access to fix problems when they occur. A niche strategy usually goes hand in hand with developing close and regular customer relationships and understanding complex and changing requirements.

2. Transactional

The second template represents a commitment to transactional superiority – i.e. to do outstandingly well at the point of sale where others might do adequately. Organisations adopting this template are often in price-sensitive markets where customers tend to shop around and service may be the key differentiator. Here we would recognise Marks & Spencer as just such an organisation. Marks & Spencer operates in a crowded, mature food and clothes retailing market but achieves its edge by quality guarantees and the ability to recover quickly from product or service problems.

3. Niche

The third template is for those who choose to identify a highly segmented customer group and then go to great lengths to understand fully and satisfy the needs of that group. In their 1993 *Harvard Business Review* paper, Trecy and Wievsema refer to the development of such a relationship as 'customer intimacy'.

First Direct, the UK telephone banking service, well fit this category. Their outstanding success is due to careful identification and management of a customer segment drawn from professional people. Such a group usually need to conduct their banking arrangements out of conventional office hours and may require relatively complex transactions to be carried out efficiently and with total reliability.

HOW AN ORGANISATION WOULD DEMONSTRATE ITS SERVICE STRATEGY

The original service strategy will have been developed from a vision; a mission by which to achieve that vision; and a philosophy to enable the organisation to carry out its mission.

An excellent example of a vision can be seen at Merrill Lynch, one of the world's most respected merchant banks. Their aim is to make all their employees aware that their corporate culture is the sum total of how they conduct themselves. In other words, 'It is who we are' that counts, and how the firm will be remembered.

Merril Lynch have established five core principles to underline their corporate culture. They are client focus, respect for the individual, teamwork, responsible citizenship and integrity.

Elsewhere, an oil company running a network of service stations has stated its vision as enabling motorists to refuel their cars with the minimum of fuss. Their philosophy is therefore to provide a network of fast, friendly, safe and clean service stations and to ensure that each of these attributes can be measured for its effectiveness.

In order to benchmark a competitor we need to examine the individuality of its service strategy and view it against that of our own organisation. We also need to assess how well its strategy is followed through to customers in practice. For example, in the case of the service station network, do their sites actually appear clean? How does the speed of their service compare with ours? Are staff friendly?

We would sum up this section on benchmarking service strategy with these key points:

- Does the vision appear visionary? For example, does it look to the future or does it assume merely a continuance of the past?
- Are the characteristics or philosophies an accurate reflection of their vision?
- Is the service philosophy distinctive in any features and is it based on all the available researched customer understanding?
- Would customers be able to notice the service attributes detailed in the strategy? Can the attributes themselves be benchmarked?
- Is there a single overriding theme for which customers recognise this organisation? If so, is the theme reflected in the strategy?
- What do we want our enterprise to be famous for?

BENCHMARKING CULTURE

To a major extent, an organisation's culture will determine the success or failure of engineering a customer-focused ethos. Being an evocative subject, cultural issues are perhaps the most difficult aspect to modify in organisations which wish to bring about change.

There are three types of organisational culture in terms of attitude to customers (illustrated in Figure A):

- customer arrogant culture;
- customer complacent culture;
- customer passionate culture.

It is worth drawing a brief picture of each of these three cultures before moving into more detail about how they can be benchmarked.

CUSTOMER ARROGANT ORGANISATIONS

Customer arrogant organisations believe they are God's gift to the market. Whatever has gone wrong is never their fault. Customers are viewed with suspicion, and are blatantly guilty until proved innocent. Such companies are never prepared to put themselves out for you. In

Figure A The three tribes

the early days of Ford Motors, their so often quoted 'only in black' offer was an example of such a culture.

In another example, one of my colleagues had a cup of coffee accidentally spilled over his jacket by an Air France stewardess. Once he had noticed the stain he complained to the cabin steward who immediately responded that it must have been there before he boarded the flight. Battling against downright rudeness and arrogance and repeated statements that they were not at fault, he dug his heels in and escalated the matter up to the president of the company. Finally he managed to extract a letter of apology with a small compensation.

According to Robert Heller, writing in the *Journal for Quality and Customer Excellence*, IBM may have qualified for the category of customer arrogance. 'The perceived internal needs had taken precedence over the unperceived requirements of the customer', he writes. 'In the words of a colleague who was a data processing manager of a multinational, IBM "told you", in your position as customer, what was best for your data processing department. If you, merely the DP manager, disagreed then they soon escalated the issue to the Vice President.'

Blind to what may have been appropriate for the customer, they fought damned hard to get their new mainframe or upgrade because that's where the margins were. Not to mention that's where the salesperson got his/her greatest reward. Customers were merely an inconvenience. At 'Not So Big Blue', of course, all that has now changed, and their customer-response programmes are up with the best. It's a shame that the cold hard reality of plummeting profitability brought about their change in attitude, and we hope it has not been too late.

We know that less that 2 or 3 per cent of the people who are dissatisfied with a service actually take the trouble to complain. In this respect, Europeans are particularly poor complainers. The vast silent majority just wait until some other organisation comes up with a better offering and then take their business elsewhere at the appropriate time. Witness the 400,000 customers who have already joined up with First Direct, the new UK direct banking service. So successful has been the offering that First Direct advertisements promote vigorously the number of account holders who defect to them each month. The organisation claims to offer independently audited customer satisfaction levels more than twice that of any UK clearing bank or building society.

CUSTOMER COMPLACENT ORGANISATIONS

Customer complacent organisations believe that their historic strengths in the market will carry them through. They remain oblivious to the fact that customers keep leaving them for their competitors and completely fail to realise that a particularly aggressive new entrant into their market would probably bring about mass defections of their 'historically loyal' customers.

When you complain to them about a service issue, you are dealt with superficially. Initially the response might seem to express concern, but follow through is weak or non-existent. Such companies do not understand the needs and requirements of their customers and make no effort to do so. They rely entirely on external market research specialists to talk to their customer on their behalf rather than doing so themselves. These are organisations which defend with vigour and passion that their customers are firmly in mind but in reality are about as far off the mark in meeting their needs as Sinclair was with his electric trike.

For example, a spokesperson for the UK Banking Association was on the radio the other day defending the high standards of service offered by the UK clearing banks following a recent consumer report of 3,000 customers which had observed that customers were not happy with the service they received. The banking spokesperson's argument was that only 10,000 customers had referred cases to the banking ombudsman, which was statistically unrepresentative of the millions of customers served. What was not raised was the effort that one has to go through to refer a case to the ombudsman. Most people don't even know they have the right to do so or know how to go about it. Imagine the result if such formal representations were easier to make!

I would put most of the European retail banks in this customer complacent category, with particularly bad examples in state controlled markets. Also, many insurers fall into this category. How many times can you recall an insurance representative calling you up to see if you might be renewing your premiums and soliciting your views on the service received over the last year? Far from it. The usual communication is the receipt of an impersonal form letter and requote for the new premium, totally assumptive that you will be renewing your premiums automatically for the following year. Most insurance policy holders are confused between the role of the broker and the insurance provider, and I'm not at all sure that either knows who their customers are.

Although I may not make many friends with my own colleagues from the auditing profession, I would submit that most of the big six audit firms are guilty of customer complacency. Shielded by the annuity of a regular audit they assume that the client organisation is satisfied with the service on offer. Often the *status quo* remains until a new financial controller is appointed and the business goes out to a re-audit. I must recognise that auditors have a particularly difficult job delivering satisfaction as their audit teams have to work hard at adding value to a service which is, in marketing terminology, a 'distress purchase'. Statutory rules dictate you have to be audited and I would reckon that without such rules many organisations would not choose to suffer such an audit.

CUSTOMER PASSIONATE ORGANISATIONS

Customer passionate organisations are those which have decided that customer focus is the key criterion for success. Following their difficulties in the 1980s Motorola have made quite a significant comeback through the introduction of, and the commitment to, a major customer-focus programme.

The Motorola six-sigma programme has set the objective to delight 99.99 per cent of customers and even the infrequent failure is followed up ruthlessly. Senior management regularly meets with customers independently of the sales teams and as one of them commented to me, 'everyone in the senior team has been in the front line with customers at some stage of their career. The customer and their satisfaction is steeped in our culture'.

Part of the staff remuneration at Motorola is based on customer satisfaction. Data recording this is collected from a variety of sources which include independent audits. Employees not normally in the front line with customers visit their premises. Financial and customer satisfaction data are both given equal weighting at management meetings and as evidence that customer responsiveness is an essential ingredient to good financial performance, Motorola's profitability grew by 120 per cent last year. Even their annual report has a section devoted to their customer programme.

The other organisation that gets my vote for customer passion is the Patel family newsagents just around the corner from where I live. Mr Patel knows all his customers by name and can recall their reading preferences. He will do literally anything to please his customers including taking in dry cleaning when the shop next door is closed and even keeping an eye on things while you're away from home. This is in exchange for the assurance that I will keep on spending £8.50 a week on newspapers and magazines!

FROM ARROGANCE TO PASSION

Much of my recent consulting work has been devoted to providing organisations with a route map for changing the culture of their organisations toward a style that is more concerned with delighting customers. I consider benchmarking to be a major mechanism to help bring about the necessary change and the rest of this chapter is concerned with how organisations can benchmark their own culture against the model they would most like to emulate.

I will suggest a means of finding where your organisation stands in the continuum from arrogance to passion. We will see how you can learn from companies which are obsessed with delighting customers and we will develop a means for helping you track your progress towards a more customer-focused organisation.

ASSESSING YOUR CUSTOMER CULTURE

Benjamin Schneider, a US researcher, has developed the use of a tribal model for assessing the culture of organisations. I have adapted this model to help assess the customer culture in your organisation and to identify the changes which need to be made to make your company customer-focused.

The recognition that tribalism exists not only in primitive cultures but also in modern organisations has been gaining some acceptance amongst management researchers. Organisational tribalism brings out deeply ingrained behaviour in people and is often the result of several generations of programming. Asking a tribe to change its behaviour may be akin to getting a leopard to change its spots and, in this context, many managers have taken on the job of culture change without first appreciating the enormity of the task ahead.

Anthropologists have categorised tribes as having four key attributes: rites, rituals, totems and rules.

Rites

Examples of organisational rites would be promotion, training and recruitment. Promotion, or the annual assessment or payround circus is perhaps the most significant rite of modern organisations because it validates the individual's contribution. Consider your own organisation for a moment. Who tends to get promoted – the bean counters, the techies, the smooth talker or the account manager with the most satisfied customer portfolio?

Rituals

Rituals are important to organisations as they mark significant events and enable a common bond to develop among participants. Retirements, inductions, celebrations of promotions or the darker aspect of the 'corridor whisper' when someone has to leave unexpectedly, are well known rituals with which we have become familiar. Again, looking at your own company, how often do customer heroes get to be celebrated?

Totems

As the badge would suggest, totems are symbols of what the organisation stands for. It may be the corporate HQ, or the portrait of the founder President, or the award-winning trophy, or the mission statement. Each speaks volumes in terms of the meaning it conveys. Do any of *your* totems reflect customer values? If you installed a totem for customer value at your company, would the portrait of the President still overshadow all else?

Rules

Last, but by no means least, written and unwritten rules define acceptable and unacceptable behaviour in an organisation. There will be rules governing sales calling for both senior and junior sales staff, rules for reporting results, rules for convening meetings and rules for chasing bad debt. Does your organisation express any rules governing the way customers will be handled in as clear a manner as those concerning internal matters? The answer is probably not.

We will continue by taking a more detailed look at how these four key attributes of rites, rituals, totems and rules differ between the customer arrogant, customer complacent and customer passionate tribes. As we develop the picture, try to identify which stereotypes conform most to your organisation.

TRIBAL STEREOTYPES IN CUSTOMER ARROGANT ORGANISATIONS

Common rites in customer arrogant tribes

A well-known rite in a customer arrogant organisation is the worship of hierarchy. Every week or month (often called 'prayer meetings') the faithful (the management team) gather to hear the boss (God) hold a one-way conversation. Chins on chest, these disciples listen in silent awe-inspired adoration. Usually, promotion is awarded to 'bag carriers', and frontline personnel who constantly put customers before organisational directives are considered odd-balls generally never to be promoted to levels of authority. Such an organisation has a continual succession of managers doing their usual two-year stint while on the route to the top, none of whom appreciates the value of long-term customer relationships.

Figure B 'Madam, if you don't like what we sell, then I suggest you sod off and find someone else's time to waste....'

- When customers leave and take their business elsewhere, a 'good riddance' attitude prevails. No one asks them why they defected, nor has anyone bothered to find out. There are plenty more where they came from.
- When a major account is lost, the event is hushed up. Usually 'they couldn't afford us' is given as the official reason, and most customer losses are put down to price.
- The organisation has little idea how many customers defect every year for competitor offerings.
- New customers who decide to buy products and services are considered 'wins' but never asked the reasons for their purchase decision or if their expectations are being met.
- People who get promoted to the top are seldom 'customer heroes'. Promotion is more likely for administrators and 'control freaks'.
- New strategies or plans are unveiled with an element of the 'emperor's new clothes'. No matter how absurd or irrelevant they may be from a customer's perspective, everybody must praise the new direction.

- Little training is given to new recruits or employees on customer understanding. It is assumed that this is something they will pick up as they go along.

Common rituals in customer arrogant tribes

Common rituals are the celebration of achieving sales targets, often at the expense of compromising customer needs. These sales targets are predominantly aimed at keeping shareholders satisfied that income continues to grow steadily upwards. Salespeople have been known to book sales, not really committed, to meet quarterly targets, thereby artificially inflating financial performance. Every now and then there is a ritual 'hanging' when someone doesn't meet these targets. Sales conferences are usually full of razzamatazz without a customer in sight. The faithful rally to the call to 'go out there and get them' by drowning themselves in a surfeit of booze and inflated egos.

Figure C 'Well done Fred. Only you could have sold those bad eggs. Now take a bit of rest before going back to serving the punters.'

- Achieving or exceeding sales targets is celebrated with great pomp even though customer satisfaction with the organisation may be wholly inadequate.
- Customer complaints are taken seriously only when legal action is threatened. Then the problems are fixed at great cost and huge management effort.
- The sales force visit customers to tell them what they need. There is an obvious expression of annoyance if customers disagree with this regime.
- Customers are rarely involved in strategy formulation or rationalisation programmes. Customers would most likely be shocked by what they might see inside the organisation.
- If and when customers are surveyed, it is usually by third parties whose findings are rejected if they are unfavourable to the management's perceptions of things.
- Sales conferences are 90 per cent about new products and how they should be sold. Usually these commandments on product sales campaigns come from out-of-date and out-of-touch marketing functions.
- Management meetings are dominated by internal issues, many of little significance to customers.
- Management rarely visit or meet customers. In truth, most of them are actually frightened of customers.
- Customers are never allowed in at Board meetings. 'We wouldn't want to wash our dirty linen in public' is the excuse.
- The annual sales plan is arrived at by taking last year's and adding 10 per cent. The plan is usually product driven rather than by customer needs.

Common totems in customer arrogant tribes

In keeping with the worship of power and hierarchy, the most common totem to be found is a picture of the leader as a constant reminder to the tribe of who is in control. Often, there will be a hall of fame with pictures of past incumbents. Traditional values are

Figure D 'Thanks for the job Guv'. We all know who's the most important person around here.'

strongly emphasised through branding and customers are given clear messages that this organisation is not for change. In certain circumstances such an organisation may be able to trade quite successfully for some time on the snob value of this timeless image. But generally it will not last as long as devotees expect.

- Pictures of the Chairman or President adorn places of prominence to remind employees who pays their salaries and he usually resides in an ivory tower HQ which, coincidentally, matches the arrogance of the tribe.
- The only reserved space in the car park is for the President or Managing Director.
- Fancy titles abound, none of which means much to customers but have great significant to the organisation.
- The sales force are considered to hold primacy on all customer issues, while other frontline teams are disregarded or considered unimportant.

Common rules in customer arrogant tribes

The rules of the tribe are articulated via written procedures but more often than not it is the unspoken rules that actually dominate behaviour. Rule number one of the unspoken variety is the primacy of the individual. Next comes the continuance of the tribe and last, and definitely least, the needs of the customers. The tribe is governed by strictly compartmentalised job functions and if you are in selling, then that is all you do. Credit chasing is done by accounts receivable and the clerk in accounts might well go to great lengths to destroy your customer relationship because an invoice is one day overdue and there are 'debtor days' targets to meet.

These organisations do not accept, recognise or tolerate failure. Chip Bell, who teaches an excellent course called 'Managing knock your socks off service', comments on Exxon's handling of the Valdiz disaster: '... To many of Exxon's customers, the memory of the Valdiz disaster seems to this day an unforgivable mistake. Their delay in making a credible response and an abrogation of responsibility for

Figure E 'Can't you read? We close on the dot of 4. Come back tomorrow. Maybe we'll serve you then...'

the disaster was perceived by customers as a disregard for them'. Contrast this with the way Perrier recovered from the traces of benzene found in their bottles or how the cyanide incident in Johnson & Johnson's Tylanol is seldom mentioned.

This is a summary of some of the common rules in customer arrogant tribes:

- Management and employees put themselves and the organisation before the customers.
- Frontline job functions are strongly compartmentalised with a great separation between feuding sales and marketing tribes.
- Customers are an inconvenience.
- The first assumption is that customers are wrong unless they can prove themselves right.
- The remuneration of the sales force is based only on sales. There is no element of customer satisfaction in the earning potential.
- Only financial data is used for reviewing business progress and monthly sales reporting.
- Failure is punishable by sacking or financial penalties.
- The organisation has no means of valuing long-term customer relationships. Account managers with such relationships are seen as 'odd-balls'.

TRIBAL STEREOTYPES IN CUSTOMER COMPLACENT TRIBES

Common rites in customer complacent tribes

The most common rite in these tribes is the continual restructuring or tinkering with the organisation. Customers are rarely involved in these processes and the primary motivation for them is inevitably reduction in costs rather than provision of added value to customers. Invariably, frontline teams are paired back while head office roles seem to stay largely intact.

- When a major customer takes their business elsewhere all hell breaks loose. It usually comes as a total surprise to the organisation.

Figure F 'See that customer over there? He's been buying here for years. What have you done to upset him, you fool?'

- Lost accounts are sometimes followed up by calling on the customer, but any analysis is frequently lost once the hue and cry has died down. Points of action are rarely incorporated into the way these organisations handle their customers.
- The organisation states that it would like to know the rate at which its customers are defecting elsewhere, and is concerned about its potential effect on profitability. But it hasn't really tried hard to work out how to measure it.
- New customer 'wins' are celebrated widely and tend to be valued more than existing customers who repeat a purchase.
- The organisation recognises successful customer heroes but usually 'promotes' them out into functions which have little to do with customers in the future.
- New strategies are unveiled with some criticism for their relevance to customers. Some amendments are made where significant gaps exist.
- Customer awareness is seen as a training need which fulfils an obligation once administered. Success of these training programmes is

measured by the number of employees attending rather than the resulting effectiveness of the training on servicing customers.

Common rituals in customer complacent tribes

The most frequent rituals celebrated are product launches or the roll-out of some new strategy. It is very unlikely that customers have been closely involved in the development of any of them, and invariably when these new products and strategies fail they are followed quickly by yet another round of new launches.

- Missed sales targets are often reconciled as the result of the 'tough market conditions' at the time. There is minimal analysis of the true reasons.
- When customers complain there is a flurry of activity and copious promises. But they are soon broken because the organisation is unable to respond quickly to fix the problem.

Figure G 'Every year this happens. Trade takes a dive. Nothing to worry about. They all come back when they realise what they're missing.'

- The sales force visit customers ostensibly to listen to what they say they want, but then respond with products and services which were not asked for.
- Sometimes customers are involved in product development and strategy formulation, but because the R&D department is a law unto itself very few of the customer-oriented ideas are incorporated.
- These organisations spend vast amounts of money on market surveys. They believe that the more you survey the customer, the more you understand them. But sadly most of these surveys are unco-ordinated, so they confuse the customer and produce little in the way of actionable information.
- Generally speaking, sales conferences are about new products. Rarely have key customers been invited to talk about their organisations and describe how and why they have been using the company's products and services.
- Managers and staff keep saying that internal meetings should contain more discussion about customer issues but this never actually happens.
- Management visit customers on an *ad hoc* basis but their visits are not co-ordinated with frontline teams and are usually with old service or college colleagues from way back.
- The sales plan is developed in classic 'bottom up', 'top down' fashion. However when the 'bottom up' numbers don't look encouraging management change them.

Common totems in customer complacent tribes

The most prominent totem erected by these organisations is the head office building. Usually located in one of the more expensive parts of the country, it is often unjustifiably expensive except that it's within easy commuting distance for the directors and its opulence is intended to signal to the market that the company is doing well.

- Throughout the office buildings there are framed slogans or quality statements. Unfortunately, no one knows what they stand for and in any event staff would have to be rather smart to even understand the meaning of the splendid adjectives used.

Figure H 'With all these new signs, our customers will realise they're going to get a better service'

- When key customers visit the office, their names are announced on the information board at reception. While this is intended to make them feel special and signal the relationship to employees, its effect on other customers visiting that day is to make them feel distinctly less privileged.
- Key customers are given special managers to manage the account. Unfortunately, there often appears to be more than one (and indeed sometimes several), each of whom tells the customer that he has this role and thereby creates confusion and doubt.
- The organisation thinks it believes that the sales people and all other frontline teams share equal responsibility for customers. However the belief is not shared by the sales staff, who recognise their isolation.
- Following a change initiative, the 'new', 'more efficient' and 'responsive' organisation is promoted extensively to customers but they seem unable to spot the difference from the previous one.
- Somewhere in the mission statement there lurks the word 'customer', but only because it's fashionable to do so.

- The organisation doesn't know the position of its offer with regard to competitors.

Common rules in customer complacent tribes

The organisation has a whole host of rules which have evolved over a period of time, although most employees don't know them. Customers find that if they want something done, and are prepared to be persistent and escalate the issue up the ladder then perhaps they will get what they want. Sometimes strong relationships develop between account management teams and customers but the organisation frequently intervenes by moving the key players on to either management roles or bigger responsibilities, often without any consultation with customers.

One client of a major audit firm commented to me, 'When we get a manager who we get on with, he usually is successful in picking up additional work. But we can be sure that once his success is recog-

Figure I 'Don't let him get away with it. He's obviously dropped that and broken it. Just give him 5% off.'

nised (by the firm) he is pulled off the account because they want to see if he can do the same elsewhere'.

- A few people put the customer first and the organisation 'allows' them to, provided they don't upset too many internal functions.
- A few of the frontline jobs have been defunctionalised but most of the larger more powerful 'baronies' still remain.
- On the whole, customers have been recognised as important stakeholders in the organisation's success. Frontline teams believe it with a passion, but management are less committed.
- When a customer complains or returns goods the organisation accepts it and resolves it first time. However, few arrangements exist to ensure this doesn't happen again.
- The remuneration of the sales force and management team is based to some degree on customer satisfaction data. However, the organisation cannot agree on the appropriateness of the measures used.
- Non-financial, customer-driven parameters are used to monitor the business, but the financials are in the majority and are the only ones which people appear to accept and understand.
- Failure is punishable by being given a job on 'special projects' or in marketing.
- The organisation believes that long-term customer relationships are important but doesn't know how to encourage their development.

TRIBAL CHARACTERISTICS OF CUSTOMER PASSIONATE ORGANISATIONS

Common rites in customer passionate tribes

Recruitment and training of frontline personnel is a highly prized rite. For example, Singapore Airlines claim that their recruitment procedures are the most selective of any airline and that only one in every 400 applicants gets through. Further weeding out comes after an intensive training programme. Training in serving customers is given equal weighting to the training which pilots need to fly the planes or the technical updates ground engineers require to maintain them.

Figure J 'It's been a great pleasure serving you. But now that you are leaving for Mars we won't be able to help you. Until, of course, we open our new office there...'

Back to the example of the Patel corner shop newsagent. Under the watchful eye of Patel senior, the children first learn to serve customers only at weekends. Like artisans of the renaissance, through their early initiation they will learn the customer value cherished by their parents.

- When customers leave and take their business elsewhere it is usually known and accepted by the sales team. Both customers and suppliers agree that their long-term interests are no longer served by continuing the relationship.
- In the case of an unexpected loss of a customer, the 'sudden death' is treated with great concern. Top management is always involved in finding out the causes and corrective measures are incorporated to ensure similar failures do not re-occur.
- Customer retention is measured routinely and the method of its measurement has been perfected over a number of years. The organ-

isation clearly knows which customers are worth keeping and what it needs to do to keep these customers.

- New customer 'wins' are celebrated widely but such instances are rare. The organisation has only a handful of key customers it wishes to target and may well work for years to gain their business. When they win it's a great occasion.
- The status of successful customer heroes is enhanced within the organisation by promotion to larger and more strategic accounts. In these organisations, a senior account responsibility can have more weighting than a senior management position.
- New strategies are formulated only after close consultation with customers and their announcement comes as a surprise only to competitors.
- Customer awareness training occurs regularly and employees in non-frontline functions may visit customer premises. The effectiveness of training is measured by customer feedback.

Figure K 'Now that we've all transmitted our forecasts, I see we're in for a very good millennium.'

Common rituals in customer passionate tribes

Rituals in customer passionate organisations invariably celebrate customer heroes. The company newspaper will generally feature a frontline team or individual voted by customers as their favourite for the year. At Ogilvy and Mather, for example, top account managers stay with their clients for decades. And at Motorola, senior board level executives will visit customers to check the quality of the relationship. These organisations are totally accustomed to sharing any celebrations with their customers. The sales conference, the product launch, even executive level meetings are attended by customers with whom the company wishes to share their ideas and strategies.

- Missed sales targets are rare. And exceeding targets is not the norm either. Account teams know with a good deal of precision where their revenue will come from for a long way ahead.
- When customers complain they know the correct channels to do so. The organisation encourages complaints and has clear procedures for dealing with them. These include follow-up, resolution and confirmation that the problem has been corrected.
- Sales people visit their customers regularly not only to find out what they want from the company, but also continually to check satisfaction with the offering. Proposals for new products and services accurately reflect the customer's requirements.
- No new products or services are offered without the close involvement of customers. Even R&D have a customer charter.
- Independent market surveys are seen only as a small part of the effort needed to understand customers. Company surveys together with focus groups, mystery shopper and other programmes are used to give a consolidated view of customer needs.
- Sales conferences cover not only new product announcements, but also a good deal of discussion about customers. It would be heresy were customers not invited to speak.
- All management meetings begin with a discussion about customer issues.
- Senior management are charged with visiting customers a number of times a year. Those not used to it are given training to make the programme effective. All customer calls are co-ordinated with account teams.

- The sales plan is biased towards the 'bottom up' planning process. Any discrepancy with the 'top down' numbers is checked with account teams and a consensus arrived at after hearing the customer's point of view.

Common totems in customer passionate tribes

Totems and symbols in these organisations closely reflect their mission to serve customers and are clearly communicated and understood by all staff. At the Ritz Carlton, the US hotel chain and Malcolm Baldridge winner, the corporate mission is clearly visible in all public areas – 'Ladies and gentlemen serving ladies and gentlemen'. From the courtesy coach driver to the hotel receptionist all staff dress, behave and speak like ladies and gentleman. When you thank the driver for his courtesy he replies, 'it's my pleasure, sir', rather than the usual 'no problem'. When you ask the way to the gym the attendant actually walks you there despite it being out of his way.

Figure L 'No problem whatsoever, sir. My name is Barbarella, and I will attend personally to every detail of your order.'

- The customer mission is set out simply and clearly for all to see. Everyone knows what it is, what it means and how they should apply it to their jobs. The customer mission statement is not just a plaque on the wall, but is included in most literature and communication media.
- All customers who visit the organisation are made to feel special. If customers are to be singled out for extra special courtesies then this is done discretely.
- There is only one key account manager. Everybody is aware of that person's role and ensures that all communication with the customer takes place with the account manager's agreement or knowledge.
- All members of the frontline team believe they have equal responsibility for the customer. The sales people see themselves as the identifiers of customer needs rather than 'product pushers'.
- During any change programme, account teams keep in touch with customers to ensure that the 'new' organisation will improve life for the customer.
- The organisation emphasises to customers its virtue of flexibility and responsiveness to change.
- Competitors are respected and benchmarked regularly to establish competitive position.

Common rules in customer passionate tribes

The rules of customer passionate organisations are best summed up in this sentiment from the Chief Executive Officer of NADT, a US company: 'If the customer wants his order wrapped up in a paper bag and delivered during a full moon then that's what we'll do. You know why? 'Cos we like to eat'. If customers complain, then they are listened to and the problem is fixed quickly and confirmation sought later that they are happy with the resolution. Marks & Spencer pioneered the 'no questions asked' return of goods in an era when the assumption of most other British retailers about their customers was one of mistrust.

Stew Leonard, the US retailer which claims sales per square feet twice the national average, has a plaque in every store which reads,

Figure M 'Look, I hear everything you say about this, but we can't let the customer down. Let's go on the video link now, and find out how to fix it.'

'Our policy is: No. 1 the customer is always right. No. 2 If the customer is wrong read rule No. 1'.

At Rank Xerox, substantial weighting is given to customer satisfaction in remuneration and promotion. The company has a complex set of customer satisfaction criteria which will contribute up to 30 per cent towards determining the bonus for the sales force. Customers get to know that the people serving them are being evaluated on the quality of service and can develop an unspoken but strong ownership in the salesperson's success. There's many an example in the friendly Manhattan waiter who gets the biggest tips and then one day ends up running the bar.

Unlike customer arrogant organisations where strict hierarchical management only allows the frontline team to service the customer within narrowly defined boundaries, the customer passionate organisation encourages them to take all reasonable decisions without reference up the management chain. In addition, this organisation will have substantially reduced its focus on job functions, and instead will have designed jobs around the customer. The same person will be equally capable of taking your order or answering an invoice query or arranging for someone to call round for a maintenance check.

Customer understanding is highly valued and these organisations use numerous channels to gain it. In addition to commissioning external research they also capture intelligence from the sales force, service teams, delivery units and complaints handling systems.

Proctor and Gamble, for example, detected through their complaints hotline that their consumers were increasing the frequency of their washes. They concluded that the reason for this was that more garments were being sold with varying washing temperatures. In an environmentally responsible gesture, the company launched 'All Temperature Cheer' as a result. Customer passionate organisations work closely with customers in the development of new strategies and products.

- Everybody has to put the customer first. Everything is scheduled around the customer. The quickest way to get things done is to say 'it's for a customer'.
- Although some functions exist, the unifying mission of meeting customer needs ensures co-operation across traditional functions. Instead, most of the organisation is structured around processes.
- Everybody acknowledges that customers are the bloodline to the organisation. If anybody forgets it they are treated as 'outcasts'.
- Customer complaints are seen not only as a problem event which must be resolved quickly and satisfactorily, but also as an opportunity to understand the customer from the ensuing interaction and improve performance in the future.
- Customer satisfaction measurement is the prime mover behind all remuneration schemes. The organisation fully understands the potential contribution of individual job roles to enhancing customer satisfaction.
- Non-financial measures of customer management are seen to be key drivers to financial performance and the organisation has established the relationship between the two sets of data. Both are reviewed regularly.
- The organisation expects people to learn from failure. Those that don't are asked to leave.

Characteristics		Customer arrogant (High – Low)	Customer complacent (High – Low)	Customer passionate (High – Low)
Rites	Comp A	□	▒	■
	Comp B	■	□	□
	Comp C	▒	■	□
	Comp D	□	▒	■
Rituals	Comp A	▒	■	□
	Comp B	■	▒	□
	Comp C	□	■	▒
	Comp D	□	□	■
Totems	Comp A	□	▒	■
	Comp B	■	□	□
	Comp C	□	▒	■
	Comp D	□	□	■
Rules	Comp A	▒	■	▒
	Comp B	■	▒	□
	Comp C	▒	■	□
	Comp D	□	▒	■

■ Exhibits strong traits ▒ Exhibits few traits □ Exhibits little or no traits

Figure 2.2 Templates to help you plot your own organisation's culture in comparison to others. It is unlikely that any organisation will conform entirely to one particular tribal stereotype, hence you score areas where strong traits exists against areas where only weak or non-existent evidence exists. Company A, for example, shows a strong concentration of customer passionate rites with a few traits of complacency. The high/low scales position Company A within the three stereotypes. Company A is making the transition from complacence to passion, while Company B has its feet firmly in the arrogant camp.

- Long-term relationships are encouraged and people's status generally reflects the strength of these relationships.

SO WHERE DO YOU STAND?

You will probably find parts of your tribe in each of the categories described. Should you recognise most of the customer-passionate traits in your company then have no fear for the moment. However, few companies today conform to this model and those that do are nearly always more profitable than their competitors. If complacency and, worse still arrogance, are closer to home then you should start doing something about it soon.

Where do you think your competitors stand? If they're all about as complacent and arrogant as you then perhaps just a small culture shift will begin to give you an advantage. But if the tables are reversed and you are the arrogant organisation then you've got a major programme of change ahead of you.

To become more customer-focused will not be achieved by introducing slogans or assuming that an organisation can easily reverse decades of cultural behaviour. Significant changes to all four tribal characteristics described may well be needed if we are to bring about the necessary change.

Unfortunately, tribes have historically only changed in response to a crisis. Palaeolithic man changed from hunting to farming only after significant changes in climate. IBM needed a $5.5 billion loss to dramatically change its culture. For many others change came too late.

The grid in Figure 2.2 may be useful to help you plot your culture position with regard to competitors and determine what characteristics you need to change.

BENCHMARKING SKILLS AND COMPETENCIES

Employees in frontline roles who serve customers require competencies which may not normally be nurtured in the commercial world. Often we attempt to provide training to frontline teams to enable them to take on some of the competencies required to serve customers.

Customer service involves interaction between people and possibly the best examples of professions which display these competencies exist outside the world of business. For example, consider as one of the competencies for customer service people the need for consistency of role. Customer service personnel may frequently need to handle hundreds of customer contacts a day. Each customer comes expecting to be treated with courtesy, attentiveness and a friendly, helpful attitude. People doing that kind of job need therefore to be schooled in the art of staying in an appropriate role throughout the period of contact.

While few other professions need to duplicate similar competence, actors are probably the exception. An actor needs to perform a predetermined role day after day despite how they feel. Studying the way an actor is trained must be a useful way of examining best practice to apply it to service personnel.

So we can appreciate that benchmarking competencies is not necessarily just about assessing organisations against competitors, but also about learning from parallel professionals. We now discuss a concept called 'parallel learning'.

PARALLEL LEARNING

Bill, a member of the Royal Shakespeare Company, has a degree in economics, went to drama school for five years, works for three months in the year and for the rest of his time depends upon turning up for auditions about five to six times a week. One time in twenty he gets the part, and this is a success ratio considered to be above average in London. Six times a week or so Bill puts himself on the line at an audition. As you must imagine he has learned to handle rejection well. Bill has developed an innate competence that would make most sales executives green with envy. Indeed, if Bill so wanted, he could be in sales, and would most probably be very successful and earn four times the salary. But he chooses not to do so and, in turn, commercial organisations haven't even considered the prospect of employing someone like Bill as a saleperson.

Frank is a family therapist and child guidance counsellor from New Jersey. He was originally a language graduate, then trained as a therapist for three years and has for the last 15 years been in the business of dissuading suicidal kids from killing themselves. 'I use a very simple technique', says Frank. 'Initially a child referred to me is a reluctant "visitor". The second phase is to convert him into a "complainant", so he feels able to unload his baggage on me. The third and final phase is to make him a "client". In other words someone who is prepared to trust me to make them well again'.

This is an approach which many professional services firms could find useful in making clients of reluctant 'visitors'. For the past two years I have been involved in developing an approach to benchmarking best practice in professions outside the world of business. My colleagues and I have coined the expression 'Parallel learning' as descriptive of the technique which seeks to introduce mangers to learning by observing some of the key attributes of other relevant professions.

As companies compete in an environment of slow growth, innovation in customer management practices is more and more being recognised as a key battleground for the 1990s. At present most sales training for senior management is based on a collection of ageing ideas drawn from the business world and recycled every few years.

As most innovative benchmarking usually comes from a company outside your sector and provides a rich source of new ideas for best practice. So, also, parallel learning has the potential to provide a vast untapped resource from professionals using parallel competencies.

Our experience in parallel learning began in 1990 when our London based partner team at Price Waterhouse wished to develop further its ability to establish long-term client relationships. The growth in the professional services market had slowed considerably and client retention was to us a key objective.

In order to achieve and sustain client relationships we identified a series of skills which appeared to be necessary. They were: handling rejection; dealing with conflict; providing leadership; motivating staff; presenting; building empathy; counselling; listening; and understanding relationships. We reviewed many of the available traditional sales training packages and came to the conclusion that they varied from the highly structured and prescriptive to the overly evangelical. Neither of these approaches appeared appropriate to the needs of the partner group.

Our first experiment was with Frank, the child guidance counsellor I mentioned above. We asked him to spend two days with us during a retreat telling us about his work, because we figured that anyone who was able to work with despairing, often sexually abused teenagers and convert them to self-respecting individuals might well have a thing or two to offer a businessperson trying to deal with a troubled client.

His messages were delivered in *psycho speak* but were clearly interpretable for business:

- *Don't pursue a distancer.* Frank explained that a child initially coming for therapy might want to keep some 'distance' between him/herself and the therapist. Similarly, many broken marital relationships often go through a stage when one of the partners wishes to 'get away' from the other. Pursuit in these circumstances would damage any chances of mending the relationships. In the same way, pursuing certain types of customer may ruin any chances of closing a deal.
- *Look for the triangle.* Contrary to popular belief, most relationships are not simple one-to-one affairs. There is usually a third person or issue involved. For example, when teenager Sharon's relationship with her mother broke down into a highly charged and traumatic affair there was more to the simple diagnosis that her authoritarian mother insisted she spent more time at home during weekends. Analysis unearthed unwanted advances by her stepfather about which she felt unable to talk to her mother.

  A customer's motivation to proceed with a project may not be a simple decision based on the relationship between buyer and seller, but may likely involve a third factor – his boss or members of the board. In our circumstances, a complaint about fee levels or standards of service may be the result of pressures from other quarters. The astute businessperson must try to look for triangular relationships to understand the real problem rather than the one that might be immediately obvious.
- *Use a 'one way mirror'* (be a silent observer – hunt in pairs). Frank's therapist unit uses an interviewing technique which involves the use of a one-way mirror. Clients are interviewed by a therapist in a room containing a one-way mirror (with their con-

sent). A second person observes the interview from the other side of the mirror and later passes commentary on how the subject reacted in the interview session.

The second person, by observation, is able to detect subtle give-away signs in body language and speech which may pass by the interviewer. The observer and interviewer together are able to make a more powerful diagnosis of their patient than the single interviewer would have done on their own. Translated into the business world, key sales calls, for example, attended by two people can be more effective than single one-to-one meetings.

Our experience with Frank was a great success, so we decided to take parallel learning one step further with another 'parallel' profession. This time we turned our minds to the fear of rejection. To a partner at Price Waterhouse with a good blue-chip client base the idea of approaching customers to promote the firm's services would not come easy. It had become clear to us that a partner's greatest unexpressed anxiety was the fear of rejection. That's when we involved Bill the actor. By means of a series of highly interactive roleplays and exercises, Bill conveyed to us some of the key attributes of an actor's training:

- *The right to speak.* Actors are drilled in the right to say their part the way they would like despite the cold, inhospitable audition room or the hotel or the sceptical first-night audience. Knowing that one has the right to speak develops a focus of mind which can put you at a psychological advantage over the most unwelcoming listener.

  We used the right to speak in a role play to get a prospective client, who is more concerned with the issue of price, to buy in to the added value of a broader offering.
- *Centering yourself.* An actor is taught to be aware of one's body and how to get the best out of correct posture. The correct use of breath ensures you don't run out of steam at critical moments of delivery. In business we sometimes are more concerned about getting across the content rather than delivery.
- *Staying in role.* Good actors have the ability to take on the role of a

particular individual and stay within the character of that person throughout the duration of an improvisation or play. Taking on the role of an individual who helps you best cope with fear or rejection can be a useful way of coping with the most difficult customer or sales call.

Traditional training would not have been appropriate for the partner team which would have been sceptical of the usefulness of mainstream product sales education.

We took parallel learning to one of our clients, BT, one of the world's largest telecommunications companies. Senior directors wanted to make calls on key accounts as an expression of interest in customers and to signal an increased customer focus for the rest of the organisation. Parallel learning was a non-threatening way to allow senior management to observe best practice.

Experience at BT showed that parallel learning was more successful with directors who were prepared to observe best practice and make their own connections with customer management activities in their own line of business. Initially, some had difficulty with being confronted by a New Jersey psychotherapist, although the actors seemed to gain initial acceptability by using the medium of entertainment to generate interest.

In most customer service processes, personnel need to draw on competencies of which best practice examples may not always exist in the business world. Conflict resolution is an area where frontline teams handling complaints often have to incur the wrath of dissatisfied customers and engage them in a meaningful dialogue, allowing them to 'dump' their anger and frustration. Marriage guidance counsellors often handle similar situations and undergo extensive training to handle the psychology of conflict between two individuals. Their advice on the basic ground rules such as 'don't interrupt', 'let the person express their feelings' and 'acknowledge the person's feelings', can be applied with good effect to personnel handling complaints.

Alternatively, Freudian theories of parent, child and adult interactions would be equally appropriate in handling conflict situations. It was Scandinavian Air System which borrowed this thinking in the 1970s in training cabin crew to deal with irate passengers. When people complain they approximate to one of the above modes. 'I'm fed up with the way I've been treated, I want to see your manager', approximates closely to a mother telling her child,'...wait till your father comes home'. The solution, say the psychoanalysts, is to convert the interaction into an adult-to-adult dialogue. 'I feel let down and I would like the problem fixed', expresses the adult sentiment and the desired solution.

Perhaps one of the most demanding competencies of frontline teams is consistency of role. A telephone operator may have to handle hundreds of calls a day in an alert and efficient manner, a cabin stewardess may have to bid a friendly farewell to hundreds of disembarking passengers and the staff at the emergency breakdown service of your automobile association may have to show empathy and concern for a steady flow of members in distress throughout the holiday weekend. Customers catching an operator at the end of shift do not want to be treated any less efficiently than if they called four hours earlier.

Actors need to stay in a particular role night after night, often for a number of years in one of London's or Broadway's longer running performances. The actor takes on the persona of the character and trains himself to stay in the role for the duration of the play. In ancient Greek and Japanese *Noh* theatre, actors wear masks to help them take on the character they are playing. Similarly, wearing a particular uniform may help frontline teams visualise their intended role and help with consistency in customer interaction. Uniforms then take on an extended and important role not only in communicating to customers the ethos of the organisation, but also in playing an important part in helping employees with consistency of purpose.

Figure 2.3 shows a number of competencies required by customer service teams and some parallel professions which could provide best practice ideas for frontline processes.

In the next chapter we shall look at how to benchmark customer-facing processes.

Customer service competencies	Our organisation		Best practice benchmarks from parallel professions
Building empathy	Very important	Adequately met	Nurses/medical profession
Handling rejection	Very important	Poorly met	Actors
Conflict resolution	Very important	Poorly met	Marriage guidance counsellor
Counselling	Average importance	Well met	Family therapist
Understanding relationships	Important	Well met	Family therapist
Listening	Very important	Poorly met	Psychotherapist
Providing leadership	Low importance	N / A	Football coach
Communicating complex ideas	Important	Well met	Teachers
Consistency of role	Average importance	Well met	Actors

Figure 2.3 In benchmarking customer service competencies it is frequently a good idea to look at professions which typify best practice in these competencies. The process which we have called parallel learning can be adapted to train frontline personnel in emulating some of these best practice principles. An organisation needs to identify which are the important competencies and those it feels it can improve. The parallel professions may have been able to offer better insights to learning than traditional management training.

On reading this chapter you should ask the following questions of your own enterprise:

1. Have you identified which of the three service strategies you most associate with: (a) innovation; (b) transactional; (c) niche?
2. What would you like your organisation to be famous for?

- The most technically competent
- Easy to do business with
- Speed of response
- Meet all reasonable requests

3. Can you think of any other organisation which matches this description most closely?
4. Which of the tribal stereotypes do you resemble most closely?
5. Do you know of any organisation that conforms most closely with the tribal stereotype you would like to be?
6. Do you know what you need to change in order to arrive at the target culture?
7. Which of the important customer service competencies are poorly met by your organisation?
8. Are there any professions outside your sector which typify best practice in these competencies?
9. Can you visualise your most demanding and complex customer problem?
10. How do you think the most competent person in a parallel profession might resolve the issue?

Answers

1. Try not to be all things to all men. Major in one of the three categories.
2. What you want to be famous for depends on your choice in (1) above. Figure 2.1 could help you choose.
3. It's always a good idea to find a model on which to build your own service vision. To be distinctive, choose a non-competitor.
4. Use the table in Figure 2.2 to help you determine which tribal profile you correspond to. It is likely that you will find characteristics in all three templates.
5. Again as in (3) above, finding a model culture in another organisation helps you establish your target culture. You don't have to consider only companies of similar size to yours. The village store will do if it resembles in a microcosm some of the traits you want to replicate. Remember thinking 'big' but acting 'small' has fuelled change in many organisations.
6. Change the easiest things first. Rules usually take the longest because many of them are unwritten and reflect decades of behaviour.
7. Remember competencies aren't skills – they are the intuitive things we do either as a result of intense training or behavioural heritage.
8. See if Figure 2.3 is helpful in answering this.

9. We all have one to tell. Do you think you handled it well?

10. Talk over that difficult customer scenario with someone from a parallel profession and see if he or she would have tackled it differently. If you like the outcome, design some training for your customer service personnel around the solution.

3

BENCHMARKING AT THE PROCESS LEVEL

In this chapter we discuss:

- The Malcolm Baldridge European Quality Award.
- The five key customer service macro processes, and the 27 key processes.
- A case study in how Packaging International has addressed each of these processes.

This chapter will give you a chance to assess how well your company conforms to excellence at a practical level.

Many people consider process benchmarking to be the most effective form of benchmarking to help enable change in organisations. It can be of particular benefit in the following situations:

- Identifying ways to convert the organisation to being more customer-driven.
- Identifying ways in which to emulate best practice in customer management.
- Comparing one's own service organisation to others.
- Developing ways of differentiating the service offering.

Process benchmarks deal with *How to?* and lend themselves to comparisons across industry sectors. By using benchmarking processes you are able to investigate best practices from a much larger pool of organisations than would be possible by benchmarking transactions. For example, if we were to look at best practice for the process of handling complaints we may find that the way Avis handle the process in the car hire business is of equal relevance to say computer sales.

There may be several processes involved at Avis. How they provide their customer with ease of access to comment or complain; how they resolve the problems and then verify that the customer is now satisfied with the outcome; and finally, how they use the experience gained to improve their service offer. All these processes would most probably be relevant in many industries.

Managers frequently have difficulty coming to terms with process benchmarks because they tend, by nature, to be more qualitative than quantitative and consequently may require a degree of interpretation. Furthermore, process benchmarking requires a mindset that is able to make connections that may not appear obvious at first. It is unfortunate that traditional management education has not been able to teach us how to handle the ambiguity in process comparisons as a result of which our automatic impulse is to disregard their validity. Yet, in my view, the high ground in benchmarking is most definitely at the process level.

When we sought participants for our process benchmarking study we met with two different sets of responses. One set of managers commented along the lines of '... I don't see the statistical validity of processes nor do I see how my sector could possibly be compared with another ...'. On the other hand, the more process-orientated managers were heard to say '... provided you can define a set of processes that are generic to any business, then I believe we would be very interested in benchmarking ourselves with any other sectors and learn how other companies apply themselves to these processes'.

MALCOLM BALDRIDGE AND THE EUROPEAN QUALITY AWARD

Before starting out on process benchmarking we must first establish a generic framework within which to make the comparisons. The framework suggested here is based on an extract of the Malcolm Baldridge and European Quality Award for assessing customer excellent companies. At Price Waterhouse we have developed it further and it has been used as a basis for benchmarking over 50 companies so far.

The Malcolm Baldridge Award was set up in the 1980s to encourage US companies to emulate best practice towards their customers and employees. Now, more than 200,000 companies apply for the award each year and the process for achieving an award is used more as a means of improving business than actually winning it.

The European Quality Award was set up in 1991 and closely resembles the Baldridge Award with the welcome addition of 'business results'. These link the adoption of business processes with such tangible improvements as market share, customer satisfaction and profitability. The only point in emulating best practice must surely be to produce good business results.

THE FIVE KEY CUSTOMER SERVICE PROCESSES

The framework we developed is based on five key macro customer processes, illustrated in Figure 3.1:

- Understanding customers' needs.
- Managing customer relationships.
- Delivering service through people.
- Managing dissatisfaction.
- Measuring customer satisfaction.

Over the next few pages we will expand each of these macro processes into a total of 27 sub-processes and discuss how to benchmark them.

Understanding customers' needs

A full and complete understanding of customers requires the detailed consideration of three main issues (see Figure 3.2):

- Understanding near and long-term customer requirements.
- Projecting future customer requirements and expectations.
- Determining customer requirements.

Many organisations believe that good customer management begins and ends with understanding customers. And it is certainly

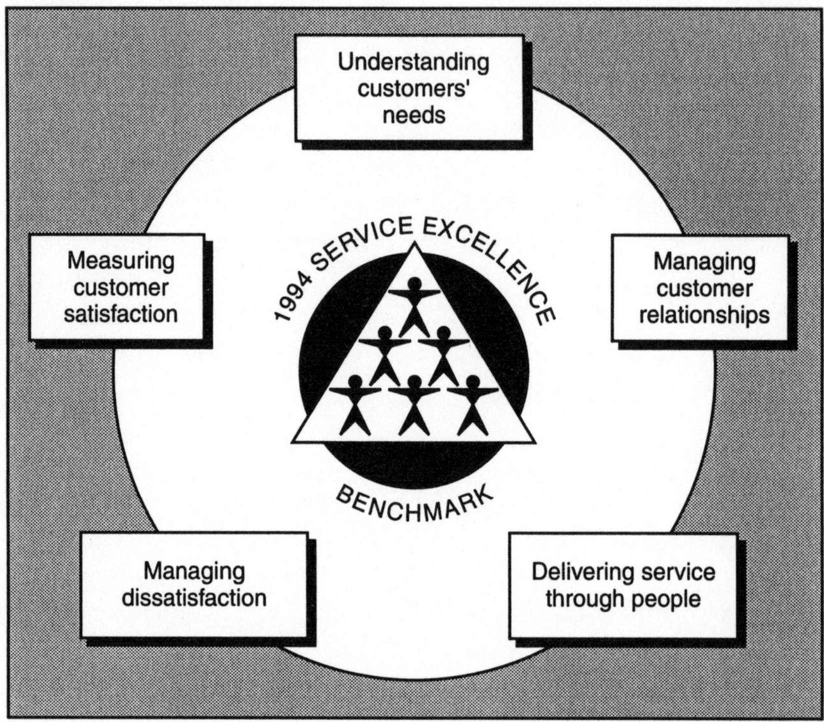

Figure 3.1 The five core customer management processes. These have been adapted from the Malcolm Baldridge and European Quality Award frameworks and have acted as the basis for a major process benchmarking study.

the case that history is littered with companies whose product and service strategies flopped and organisations which withered away because they failed to understand the needs and requirement of their customers.

Whether we pursue a service strategy to differentiate our offering or compete mainly on price, we need to have processes in place which replenish our understanding of customers on a continual basis. Sometimes we have to be masters at interpretation in order to reflect accurately our customers' needs. As one manager commented: '... customers do not always know what they need ...'. Thus it is important to combine customers' views with competitor analysis and with overall market trends to identify what might continue to motivate your customers.

Why do hotels feel the need to leave chocolate and sweets on our pillows at night before we go to bed? Why do the oil companies, year after year, promote 'me-too' gift vouchers at service stations when these junk giveaways long ceased to be an incentive? Why do retail banks persistently stay closed when customers need them most? Could it be that these organisations have failed to understand what their customers want?

Sometimes we see spectacular disasters resulting from poor customer understanding. For example, take Hoover's trans-Atlantic airline ticket offer which cost the company \$70m. The company, a UK subsidiary of US parent Maytag, promoted airline tickets worth \$600 for every \$150 purchase on the basis that few would take up the offer. In the event, over 200,000 people applied. The company was totally unprepared and intolerably slow in meeting its obligations. Frustrated customers formed an action group and took the company to court, giving rise to a great deal of bad publicity which had a damaging effect on its balance sheet.

Customer understanding is not something which is the sole preserve of the marketing department. Nor is it something for which we employ external research organisations to research and report back on. Everybody needs to be involved in understanding customers, including the management who run the company. Virgin airline's boss, Richard Branson, personally solicits comments and criticisms from upper-class passengers and reports them to this senior team. This, in itself, is both a signal to employees that everyone is involved in understanding customers and enables management to keep in touch with customer needs.

Understanding near and long-term customer requirements

Areas to examine include the following:

- *Customer groups and/or market segmentation.* We must work out the optimum way for determining these groupings. Competitors' customers and other potential customers must be considered as well.
- *The process for collecting information.* Information must be sought at an agreed frequency. The methods for collection have to be developed and the data has to be assessed for objectivity and validity.

- *Product and service features.* Each product and service has specific features, and they must be ranked individually in relative importance to customer groups or segments.
- *Determination of success.* All the information learned from complaints, gains and losses of customers and performance of the products and services must be cross-compared in order to optimise and determine success.

Understanding future customer requirements and expectations

Areas to examine include the following:

- *The time horizon for the determination.*
- *External factors which would influence customers.* The importance of technological, competitive, sociological, economic and demographic factors, any or all of which might influence customer requirements, expectations or alternatives, needs to be established.
- *Competitors.* We must try to find out how the customers of competitors and other potential customers are considered.
- *Development of new products and services.* It is necessary to know how the key product and service features and the relative market segments are addressed and their implications focused on new product and service lines as well as on current products and services.

Determining Customer requirements

- *New market opportunities.* How does the organisation evaluate its processes for determining customer requirement and expectations, and how does it relate the data to new market opportunities.
- *Time horizon for the determination.* Does the organisation adopt an acceptable time horizon to determine requirements?

We must not forget that:

1. Because products and service may be sold to end-users through intermediaries such as retail stores or dealers we must determine customer groups taking these end-users and intermediaries into account.

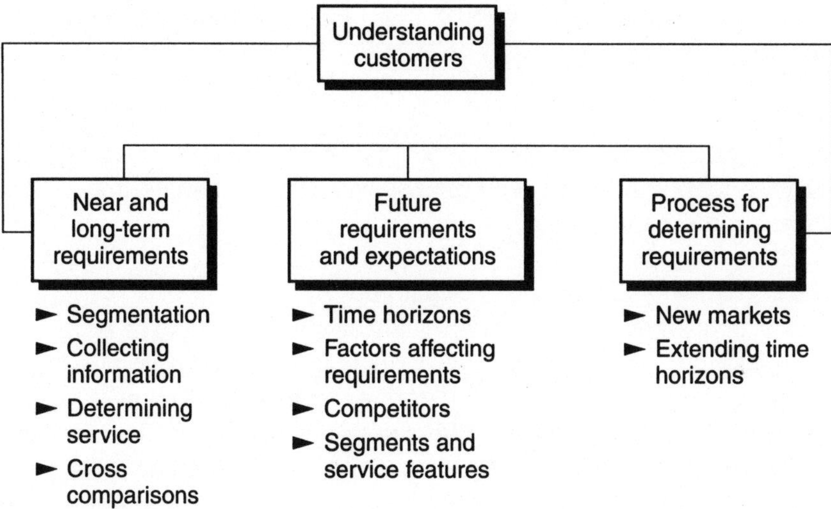

Figure 3.2 The processes of understanding customers and their associated sub-processes.

2 Product and service features refer to all the important characteristics of products and services experienced by the customers throughout the period of their purchase and ownership. These will include factors which influence customer preference and their loyalty, or their views of quality – for example, where features enhance or differentiate products and services from competing offerings.

3. Some companies will use similar methods for determining customer requirements, expectations and satisfaction. In such cases cross-references should be included.

By way of an example we will now examine a company in the packaging business to see how well it follows the process descriptions for customer understanding.

Packaging International
How they go about understanding customers

Packaging International is a company specialising in providing packaging materials. This is an extract of their process for understanding customers. See how you rate them in their ability to follow the processes described above.

We continuously review our methods for evaluating and improving our ability to meet the current and near-term customer requirements, and make improvements when warranted.

1. *Our Customers are grouped by market.*
   Our groups are food packaging, industrial packaging and re-cyclables. In each grouping we constantly monitor customer requirements and expectations through surveys, partner feedback, complaints, gains and losses of customers, product performance and trade literature. We review and prioritise these requirements to ensure that we are addressing our customers' most important requirements. Each business team or plant is responsible for prioritising and tracking action.
2. *We collect customer information using the methods described above.*
   This information is directed to the appropriate product management teams who are responsible for managing our customer relationships. The information we collect includes:

   - the product and service features most important to our customers;
   - how we are doing;
   - how our competitors are performing.

   Priorities are based on what is most important to our customers, and differences between our performance and our competitors' in these areas. Our product management teams continuously receive and evaluate customer information.

   Formal third-party telephone surveys are conducted annually of existing and potential customers. This data is formally reviewed by the business teams on a quarterly basis and verified by business team members' personal feedback from customer and market visits.

   In addition, we exhibit at various trade shows. The object of exhibiting is not only to sell products, but also to use a structured approach to gather customer-related information. After the conference, technical teams meet over a day to identify general issues and opportunities. We also use the service of a leading futures company to identify the final customers' and potential customers' future needs.

3. *Group calling.*
   Once a year, our technical marketing and technical sales groups join our major customers' technical sales group in making their sales calls. This provides opportunities to learn about our indirect customers' problems and opportunities.
   We use the processes described in (2) to determine the relative importance of our specific product and service features to our customers. Our product management teams evaluate customer feedback for items that consistently appear to be important and the 'gap' between us and our competitors in performance.

4. *Evaluation of performance data.*
   We collect and evaluate customer complaints, gains and losses, and product performance data to verify customer requirements and expectations. We recognise that our continued success depends on our ability to understand and meet our customers' future needs.
   Each of our businesses focuses on the time horizon which is most critical to its customers' future needs. While some of our Industrial and Food Packaging businesses realise they must focus on the critical time horizon of three to five years, those involved in re-cyclables are often thinking 20 years ahead. All our businesses, however, are aware of trends that will affect the plastic film business into and beyond the year 2000.

5. *External issues.*
   We deal with technological, competitive, sociological and demographic factors which may impact customer requirements, expectations, or alternatives in three major ways.

   - We have developed collaborative arrangements with the Total Quality Management, Food Science, Packaging Science and Polymeric Chemistry Programs at a leading private and a leading state university. These partnerships provide an opportunity for undergraduate students to intern in our plants and laboratories, in support of basic research in food, packaging and polymeric sciences. In addition, we have developed a mini-sabbatical program which allows an exchange of university faculty and our scientists and engineers. This program provides us with information needed to determine future technologies.
   - Each business tracks its specific global business environment factors. Our economists develop specific economic information relevant

to each business, and resources within the business keep abreast of demographic and technical trends and forecasts.

- Our RD&E resources study basic trends affecting technology and consumer patterns. One model is 'substitution'. Re-cyclables substitution for metals is only about 10 per cent underway in the US, and much less in other areas of the world. Substitution helps us understand consumer use patterns on a macro scale.

Our understanding of society's needs and technological directions enables us to design, produce and deliver solutions to specific customer long-term requirements.

6. *Competitor Evaluation.*
Through our interaction with our customer partners and their customers, we collect information about our competitors' customers and other potential customers. We then interact with these potential customers directly at trade shows, trade association meetings, and indirectly through our interactions with equipment manufacturers to determine how we could best meet their needs.

7. *Future projections.*
We project the relative importance of our key product and service features into the future:

- Through discussions of future needs between our customers and our Marketing and Technical Marketing Representatives we develop our product and service strategies.

  We hold formal meetings with our major customers' top leadership. For example, meetings with the leaders of our four largest customers are held twice a year. While these meetings focus on specific current business needs, they also address future requirements.

  Through our total customer partnership process we better understand future consumer needs. We frequently conduct focus group meetings with our customers' marketing representatives to identify consumer needs. When needs are clarified, we develop a value chain partnership, fully linking all customers from Packaging International to the retailer. This total partnership works to develop the new offering that will meet consumer needs.
- Re-cyclables uses the continuous improvements process to understand and meet new customer needs. It is based on the premise that the business exists to enable customers to design increasingly productive solutions to their own waste problems. The 'iteration'

step is where a customer team jointly identifies better ways to meet customers' needs. Critical to this process are strong partnerships formed with strategic customers.

8. *Quarterly Reviews.*
Each business segment within the company reviews quarterly its market segments for changes which might either threaten the market for existing or new products or provide opportunities for new products or services. During the review process, the business considers inputs from customers, competitive literature, government sources, trade literature and our own evaluation of other marketing data. Our technical and marketing personnel analyse these data and, at the review meetings, present a plan for addressing the changes they found.

Since understanding future customer requirements and expectations is so important to us, finding better ways to do it is built into all the approaches given above. Annually, a cross-functional team (Post Mortem Team) reviews the short- and long-term projections over the past five years, rationale for making these projections, and actual current events. Root cause analysis is conducted to determine why specific projects were not on target from either a positive or negative point of view. Strategies are then implemented to increase the accuracy of our projects.

Managing Customer Relationships

Somebody once said to me, 'In the real world only customers exist, markets are pure fantasy'. More and more organisations are beginning to abandon the concept of a market as an amorphous, faceless mass of customers in favour of moving towards the idea of establishing a relationship with customers. Those organisations that manage to forge strong relationships gain loyalty in return.

An average business traveller on an airline's frequent flyer programme may be worth up to $500,000 for the duration of his loyal relationship with the airline, while the average lifetime value of a loyal customer for a retail chain may be $250,000.

In order to introduce loyalty into these purchases, customers need to feel they have a relationship with their chosen airline or retailer.

They need to feel the organisation acknowledges them and is committed to fulfilling its promises.

In professional service sectors, relationships extend often over decades. An Ogilvy and Mather account manager once told me that he had maintained his relationship with one $50m per year account for nearly 25 years. And in the accounting world, most audit firms have a senior partner who has maintained the relationship for certain key accounts over at least a similar period of time.

There are seven steps in the process of managing customer relationships, as can be seen from Figure 3.3.

1. *Identifying key requirements.* These are the requirements for maintaining and building relationships for the organisation's most important processes and transactions that bring its employees into contact with customers. We have to establish the key quality indicators derived from these requirements and how they are to be determined.
2. *Setting service standards.* The method by which the standards that address the key quality indicators are set. How customer service strategy and standards are deployed to organisational units that support customer-contact personnel. How the organi-

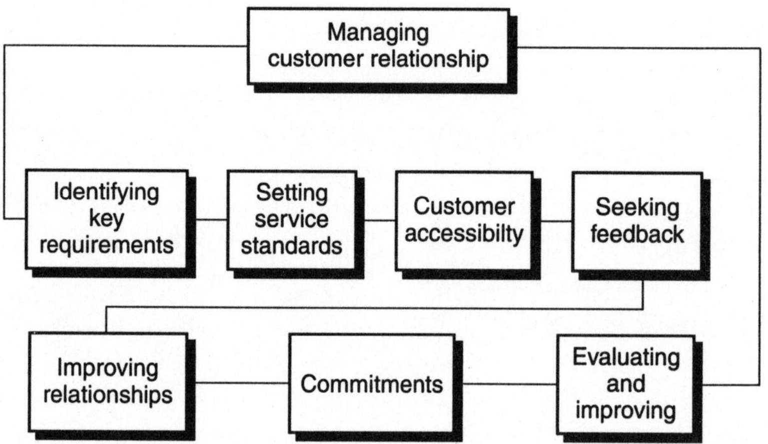

Figure 3.3 Some of the processes which make up the management of customer relationships.

sation ensures that the support provided by these units is effective and timely. And how service standards are tracked, evaluated and improved, and the role of customer-contact personnel in evaluating and improving standards.

3. *Providing customer accessibility.* The process for ensuring easy access for customers to seek assistance and to comment. We should examine the various types of contact such as telephone, personal and written, and how the organisation maintains easy access for each type of contact.
4. *Stimulating feedback.* The organisation should be seeking feedback from customers on products and services, and determine their satisfaction with recent transactions and how it will help to build customer relationships.
5. *Improving relationships.* How the organisation evaluates and improves its customer relationship management strategies and practices. We should include in this: (a) how the organisation seeks opportunities to enhance relationships with all customers or with key customers; and (b) how evaluations lead to improvements in service standards, access, customer-contact employee training, and technology support. We assess how customer information is used in the improvement process.
6. *Establishing commitments.* What commitments the organisation can make to promote trust and confidence in its products/services and to satisfy customers when product/service failures occur. How these commitments (a) address the principal concerns of customers; (b) remain free from conditions that might weaken customers' trust and confidence; and (c) get communicated to customers clearly and simply.
7. *Evaluation and improvement.* The organisation must evaluate and improve its commitments, and the customers' understanding of them, in order to avoid gaps between expectations and delivery. Points to be addressed are:

   (a) how is information/feedback from customers used?
   (b) how is product and service performance improvement data used?
   (c) how are the commitments of competitors' considered?

Packaging International
How they go about managing customer relationships

Because we sell to over 2,500 customers, we have developed relationship strategies to meet the needs of our major customers – who we see as our partners – and all other customers – small, independent and large businesses. Less than 10 per cent of our total customers account for 80 per cent of our sales volume, but sales volume alone does not categorise our customers as partners. The criteria include: customers whose market objectives are aligned with our marketing and technology capabilities; customers who are technology, product or market leaders; and customers with needs compatible with our knowledge and resources.

Personal contact is the primary means by which we determine what is important to our customers. We understand the value chain for our products, and we place resources at various parts of the chain so we can better understand customers' needs. Our marketing personnel, working with customers, define the structure of the customer relationship which is then co-ordinated by the marketing representative and supported by the rest of the organisation.

Standards are set by first researching issues important to the customer, such as the knowledge and courtesy of the associate in charge of the relationship or clarity of information. Once the key drivers have then been identified, measures are defined and tested for accuracy. Tests are conducted by the Analysis Team, and purchase trends and satisfaction trends versus the change in each key driver are tracked.

Various marketing and customer service people build and maintain customer relationships and ensure proper customer expectations relative to our products and services.

- *Account managers*, through customer relationships, develop business strategies for major customer accounts.
- *Marketing, through customer relationships*, develops business strategies to fulfil all customer needs.
- *Technical Marketing, working with customers*, identifies key products and service features which meet customer needs, provides technical assistance and seeks ways to improve our products.
- *End-Use Marketing services the downstream customer*, captures key information and reflects consumers' likely market behaviour relative to products made from our film.

> Our End-Use Marketing, Marketing, Technical Marketing and Customer Service Representatives (CSRs) build and maintain partnerships with strategic customers through regularly scheduled meetings and *Total Quality Fitness Reviews.* We also survey customers to verify our understanding of their needs and assess our performance in meeting them. In addition, Technical Marketing enhances our relationships with our customers through on-site assistance in solving problems, whatever the cause. This also helps us ensure realistic customer expectations.

The most important factors in maintaining and building customer relationships, as defined through our customer partnerships and surveys, are understanding what the customer needs; providing quality products and service to meet those needs; delivering products on time and at a competitive price; ease of access and knowledge and courtesy of associates.

In order to address those factors, we have implemented a four-step process to develop strategies and plans.

1. Customer Teams focus on specific large or strategic customers, assess their needs and business directions and develop strategies to meet them.
2. Market Teams identify opportunities and develop market strategies based on their understanding of the market needs and future directions.
3. Business Teams use input from these teams to develop business strategies.
4. Business Leaders ensure alignment with our capabilities, strategic business goals, and our customers' expectations.

Our goal is to provide easy access for customers to knowledgable, consistent contacts and to arrange regular follow-up through normal communication channels.

Our CSRs, the focal point of our day-to-day customer assistance and follow-up, are available by phone during normal working hours. We provide emergency access for our customers so they can reach us after hours and on weekends and holidays. If CSRs are unable to answer questions or address problems, they contact appropriate resources. Marketing personnel visit our strategic customers once a week and our smaller customers once a quarter. Technical Marketing representatives travel to our larger customers' plants 2–3 times per week, and they visit smaller customers as needed to deal with quality and service concerns and new product implementation strategies.

Communication with our direct customers is not limited to our primary contacts; it occurs across organisational levels. In addition to our personal contact, our businesses maintain widely advertised free phone telephone numbers to offer specific product information. We also use this contact as a source of customer information including needs/requirements.

Each business ensures that customer assistance is available when needed through a free phone telephone number, product hotline, and voice mail systems available 24 hours a day, 7 days a week. Our major customers are also connected to our electronic mail systems. Our Electrical business utilises a Call All Customers Program in which manufacturing operators at our plant phone small customers who normally would not have contact with a marketing representative.

We also maintain EDI systems which provide customers with direct access to our Product Quality Management and order entry systems. Our customers choose the communication tools which work for them. Some routinely use electronic devices, such as voice mail and/or electronic mail in their businesses and therefore feel comfortable using automated devices in their dealings with us. However, smaller companies who have fewer electronic systems prefer the personalised 'human' contact. Our customers make their preferences known through their daily contacts with us and in their survey responses.

For our largest customers, we send an electronic status report every morning to report the day's shipments, and we send additional status reports as needed through the day. When this report is received by the customer, it is reviewed. If a problem is spotted, a dialogue is initiated between the CSR and the customer to ensure that the supply will be uninterrupted.

Delivering service through people

Its a well-known fact that happy employees lead to happy customers. Front-line teams that are demoralised, low in self-esteem, in constant fear of their jobs and whose views are disregarded by managers, will not be motivated to satisfy customers.

Digital, the information technology company, have experienced falling market share through the 1990s as customers have defected to other technology providers. Many put this down to a demoralised sales force who have seen severe cuts in their numbers as the company has reduced from 130,000 employees in the late 1980s to 90,000 today. There is a perception that overheads have remained intact while the people making the sales have been eliminated. Add to that an aggressive and dogmatic style of management which does not value the views of its sales force and you have the necessary ingredients for diminishing sales. Digital has slipped from number 2 to number 3 in the sector having being overtaken by Hewlett-Packard which produces $300,000 sales per employee, roughly twice that of Digital.

There are a number of processes (illustrated in Figure 3.4) which must be considered when benchmarking the role of people in the front line serving customers:

Providing technology support

Understand how the organisation provides technology and logistics support for customer contact personnel to enable them to provide reliable and responsive services.

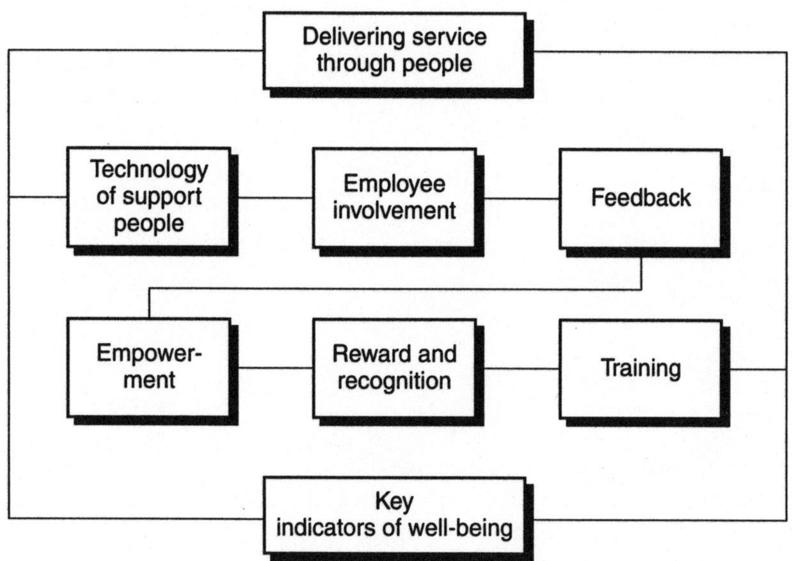

Figure 3.4 The processes for delivering service through people.

Stimulating employee involvement

Identify and improve the management practices and specific mechanisms (such as teams or suggestion systems) used by the organisation to promote employee involvement, individually and in groups. Summarise how and when the organisation gives feedback. How the motivation and involvement is achieved and sustained at all levels and functions.

Getting Feedback

Formalise the methods for the organisation to take action to increase positively its employees authority to act (empowerment), with responsibility and innovation. We need to identify the principal goals for customer contact personnel.

Allocating reward and recognition

The recognition, reward and performance measurement for individuals and groups, including managers, who support the company's customer service objectives. How is this reinforced relative to other business considerations such as schedules and financial results? How are employees involved in the development and improvement of customer service performance measures?

Training

Customer contact personnel must be trained and developed to be able to meet customer needs.

Identifying key indicators of well-being

The organisation should measure the trends in the key indicators of well-being and morale, such as satisfaction, absenteeism, and staff turnover for customer-contact personnel. We need to look for important adverse results, if any, and how problems were resolved. We should compare the current levels of the most significant indicators with those of industry averages and industry leaders.

Packaging International
How they deliver service through people

Our businesses select qualified people for customer-contact positions, provide training to ensure their success and provide the support they need.

The primary method we use to ensure a common vision for guiding customer contact associates is their experience. We continually reinforce this with our publications, including 'Quality Reports'.

1. The vast majority of our customer-contact personnel are selected from within the company. Each business identifies and selects its customer-contact personnel with assistance from our human resource consultants. Although selection factors depend on the job requirements, candidates' personnel records and work experience must demonstrate the ability to manage interpersonal and group relationships. They must possess problem-resolution skills and be goal-oriented.

   A candidate's record and peer evaluations are used to select the candidate for the job. Supervisors use *Promoting the Individual* (PTI) records, which indicate skills, interests, strengths and weaknesses, in order to screen candidates for all job openings. Where peer evaluation is used, the peer team designs questions which address specific job-related issues; and they also ask candidates to respond to a pre-defined job scenario.

2. Our customer-contact career progression paths are not linear. A person may move from manufacturing to CSR or Technical Marketing to Marketing. Career options are defined in the booklet, *Your Personal Choices.*

3. Many courses are offered to assist people in improving their relationship management skills. Such as 'Business Communications' (which includes learning telephone styles), 'Effective Negotiating', 'Effective Product Management' and 'Face-to-Face Selling'. Our 'Telephone Courtesy' course provides training in listening and talking to customers on the phone.

   Because over 90 per cent of our new customer-contact people have previous experience in the company they already have a working knowledge of our products and services. Some businesses, however, provide formal, product training for their new customer-contact associates. For example, food packaging has created classroom and hands-on training in food wrap manufacturing.

Special training sessions for new associates include a company orientation, Customer Focus Training and intensive classroom training.

Peer training is critical for all customer contact positions. The outgoing market representative or CSR will work with the replacement to help build knowledge and provide a smooth transition, which our customers have reported as extremely important to them. This transition usually takes 2–4 weeks, depending on the incoming person's skills and complexity of the new assignment.

4. We increasingly empower our customer-contact associates. Technical Marketing representatives can authorise up to $10,000 for an individual claim settlement. The CSR can set up new customers, authorise less-than-truckload shipments, initiate product returns and authorise payments up to $2,000 per incident to reimburse customers for out-of-pocket losses.

5. Associate morale is assessed informally and formally. Daily interactions with management, customers and peers provide opportunities informally to assess morale and attitude shifts and provide support. Associate morale is tracked formally through the associate Satisfaction Survey. Customer-contact data is reviewed separately as are other associate data.

6. Customer-contact associates are recognised and rewarded by peers, teams, managers, and corporate management. Every business and function has its own system of peer recognition for outstanding efforts. Monthly or quarterly recognitions include money, gifts, public recognitions and others.

   Customer Focus Awards are given annually to individuals or teams for extraordinary accomplishments in customer/market-related projects. Our program started in 1987 with ten individual awards. In 1991, four individuals and nine teams were honoured, a total of 52 individuals. For the first time, one of the honoured teams included our customers. A team consisting of winners selects the next year's winners.

7. Customer-contact positions are highly valued. Although people are reassigned within the customer-contact positions, at less than 1 per cent, turnover is low. We have established that the primary reason for leaving is promotion or career broadening.

Managing dissatisfaction

TARP, the customer research organisation, has investigated customer behaviour with regard to complaints about products or services not meeting expectations. We are not surprised to discover that in only rare instances do more than 4 per cent of dissatisfied customers complain, and in some countries such as Britain and Germany, even a lower percentage of customers complain.

Given these statistics, it would be naïve to assume that only a minority of complaining customers are dissatisfied. More likely is the assumption that vast numbers of those who do not complain simply take their business elsewhere and the supplier organisation never gets to know why.

So it must be the case that the greatest challenge at present for any organisation must be to encourage customers to complain when they are dissatisfied and provide the easiest means of access to do so. For example, why should a customer be expected to pay for the telephone call when lodging the complaint, and does he or she even have any idea whom to call?

Once a complaint has been received, then the organisation must ensure that it is dealt with quickly and to the customer's satisfaction. Furthermore, the information about the failure must be recorded and communicated with a view to eliminating a repetition of the complaint.

At Pepsi Co. they set a standard of fixing problems after just one call. ICL's complaints' handling systems have played a major part in the computer vendor's success. At Otis Elevators they have developed, over several years, an advanced customer repair answering service. They see this service as a strategic capability to keep away Japanese competitors at home and abroad. Every year they handle over a million calls from customers varying from simple requests for information to people trapped in lifts. It is never long before the contact representative has all the technical details of the installed equipment on a computer screen, and is empowered to schedule repair teams within minutes to respond to emergencies. In North America today more than 80 per cent of companies offer an 800 hotline for customers to complain.

The ability to complain easily is becoming a 'dissatisfier'. In other words, customers are taking it for granted that companies should provide adequate complaint-handling mechanisms, so much so that the process of handling complaints and rectifying problems is now vital to the maintenance of a business and its profitability. As an overall concept we should present complaints as an opportunity for improvement rather than a nuisance or threat.

Figure 3.5 charts the relationship between what the customer wants, and how the organisation might provide the solutions.

There are a number of reasons why customers complain about a product or service. They are:

- Lack of empathy from the organisation.
- No real apology is ever given.
- The bureaucracy of complaining takes time and effort.
- The cost of complaining is usually borne by the customer and in a few cases customers are even charged for fixing the problem.
- The problem is passed from department to department. No one person owns the problem.

In order to benchmark the management of dissatisfaction, the subject can be divided into five key process, as illustrated in Figure 3.6.

1. *Handling lost orders/customers.* How the organisation analyses key customer-related data and information in order to understand why customers or orders are lost.

Customer wants	Business solution
Where to go	Information
Ease of access	Telecoms/distributors
Sympathetic approach	Skills training and culture
	Technical training and information systems
Understanding of the problem	Empowerment
Fast resolution	Business processes
Minimal disruption	Preventative analysis
Not repeated	

Figure 3.5 Customer wants and solutions to customer dissatisfaction are listed.

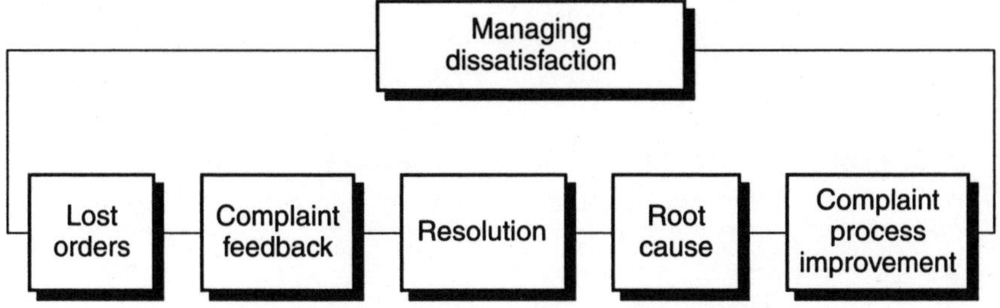

Figure 3.6 The processes for handling customer dissatisfaction.

2. *Complaint feed back.* The organisation should ensure that formal and informal complaints and their feedback are given to different company units to be aggregated for overall evaluation and used wherever appropriate throughout the organisation.
3. *Resolving the complaint.* How the organisation ensures that complaints are resolved promptly and effectively. We need to include trends and levels in indicators of response time; and trends in the percentage of complaints resolved on first contact with customer-contact personnel.
4. *Establishing the root cause.* The company should analyse complaints to determine their underlying causes. How are the findings translated into improvements? The translation may lead to improvements in processes, service standards, training of customer-contact personnel or information to customers to help them make more effective use of products and/or services.
5. *Improving the complaint process.* What are the key indicators and methods which the organisation uses to evaluate and improve its complaint-related processes? We need to understand how indicators and methods address effectiveness, response time improvement and translation of findings into improvements.

There is a significant difference between the traditional response to customer complaints and the modern best practices. For the purposes of the comparison we can categorise the overall process of managing dissatisfaction into providing the motivation to want to resolve problems, the mechanisms with which to implement the necessary resolution and the staff to undertake the job. Figure 3.7

	Traditional	Best practice
Motivation	► Legal requirements ► Warranties ► Focus on justification	► Providing satisfaction ► Retaining customers ► Visibly offering good value
Mechanisms	► Letters ► Guarantee forms ► Time-consuming	► Telephone ► Simple solutions ► Fast response
Staff	► Clerical function ► Limited authority ► Defensive/doubtful ► Limited training	► Professional (graduate trainees) ► Empowered ► Consident/supportive ► Trained and knowledgable

Figure 3.7 Comparing motivations, mechanisms and staff issues of best practice in handling dissatisfaction with more traditional values.

makes the point about how much has changed from the defensive stance taken traditionally to the more proactive open stance as exhibited by best practice.

Packaging International
How they go about managing dissatisfaction

All businesses create Problem Reports (PRs) to track complaints, status and resolutions.

1. When we receive a customer complaint, we strive to satisfy the customer and resolve the problem.

   In 1990, we computerised PRs in our businesses to store and aggregate complaint information. We do not distinguish between formal and informal complaints. All are logged and our Product Management representatives immediately begin investigation into the causes of the problems. Being held accountable for resolving complaints, they solicit input from other marketing and manufacturing resources, including obtaining and analysing samples.

Solutions are documented in the Problem Report System (PRS), and businesses track the resolution cycle time for each reported trade problem to ensure minimal elapsed time from notification to problem resolution. Each business reviews its unresolved PRs to monitor progress, assign additional resources if needed and share learning.

The computerised systems enable us to sort and aggregate complaints by business, customer, product, plant and type of problem. Trade reports are used to share our discoveries with other sites. We aggregate PR information at the business level which contains the resources accountable for its resolution. For those few large customers who buy from more than one business, data is aggregated at the customer level. A monthly summary report is generated for the business or customer.

Logging complaints allows us to monitor the number of complaints, resolution cycle time, and the claim dollars we pay out, and share our problem resolutions with other sites. An electronic problem reporting system such as ours helps us reduce the cycle time from telephone call to problem resolution and/or authorisation for product return and credit.

2. As part of the problem review described in (1) above, types and frequency of complaints are reviewed to determine the root cause and action necessary to eliminate them. In many cases, there is a direct correlation between complaints and input from customer requirements and expectations and the source of complaints received which reinforces the priority given to projects aimed at meeting customer requirements and expectations.

Measuring customer satisfaction

Many organisations take for granted that the customer is satisfied so long as the customer continues to purchase goods and services. However, the most vulnerable categories of customer to competitive threat are those who at any one moment are feeling indifferent towards the supplying organisation.

It is a sad fact that in general the vast majority of customers fall into this category and it is therefore an organisation's constant challenge to move these customers' perceptions from 'indifference' to

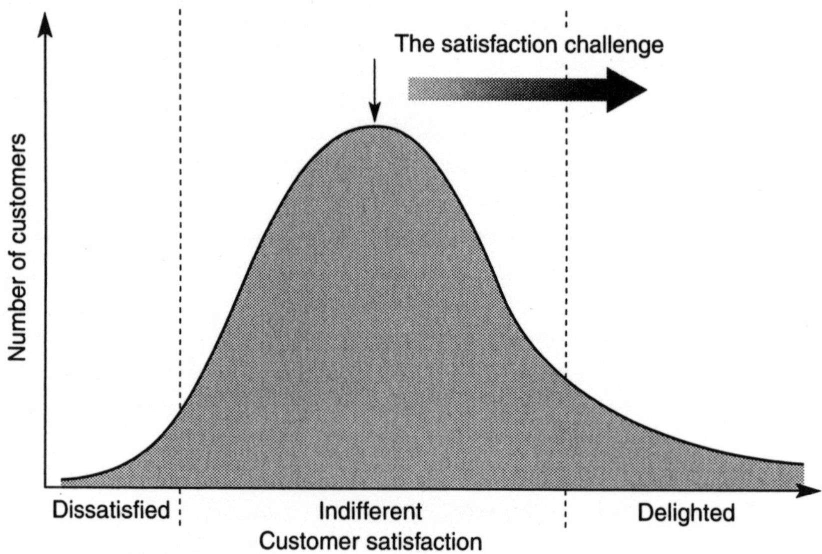

Figure 3.8 Moving customers from indifference to delight. In most enterprises the majority of customers would feel indifferent regarding their loyalty. When competing products present themselves these customers are vulnerable to switching their purchase decisions. The battle for retention needs to be fought with this group so as to increase the group of delighted customers who stay loyal. Delighted customers are achieved only via the highest satisfaction scores and therefore customer satisfaction measurement is a key indication of the success in the campaign for increased customer retention.

'delight' (Figure 3.8). We must never forget that delighted customers will be those who remain loyal. They will buy more products and services and recommend the enterprise to others. The word-of-mouth impact of loyal customers is one of the most powerful marketing devices.

Therefore, the measurement of customer satisfaction is important in order to understand the number of customers at risk from indifference, and by so doing to quantify the revenue at risk. It also helps track our endeavours to make more customers delighted with our products and services.

These are six essential processes we need to benchmark, as illustrated in Figure 3.9.

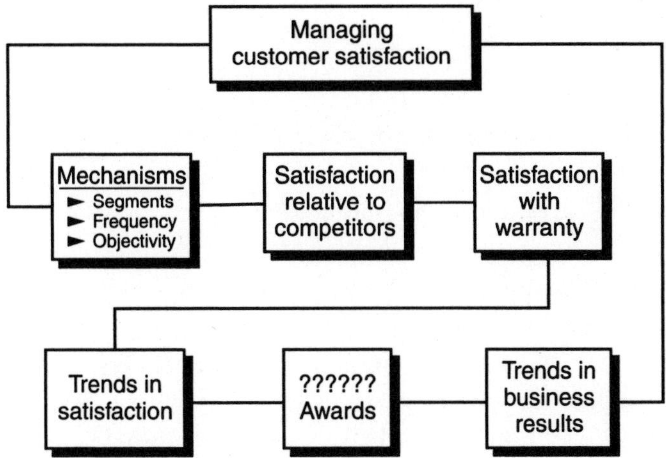

Figure 3.9 The process of measuring customer satisfaction.

1. *Mechanisms for segmenting.* How the organisation determines customer satisfaction for customer groups. We need to address: (a) brief description of market segments and customer groups; and (b) the process for determining customer satisfaction for customer groups. We include what information is sought, frequency of surveys, interviews or other contacts, and how objectivity is assured. It is all necessary to describe how the organisation sets the customer satisfaction measurement scale to capture adequately key information that accurately reflects customer preference.
2. *Measuring satisfaction relative to competitors.* The level of your customer satisfaction relative to that of your competitors should be understood.
3. *Assessing satisfaction with warranty.* Customer satisfaction and warranty/repair data should be analysed and compared with other customer satisfaction indicators such as complaints and gains and losses of customers. We will see how such comparisons are used to improve customer satisfaction determination and problem-solving effectiveness.
4. *Measuring trends in satisfaction.* How the organisation evaluates and improves its overall methods and measurement scales used in determining customer satisfaction and customer satisfaction rela-

tive to its competitors. There are several ways that trends in satisfaction should be monitored.

- Trends and current levels in indicators of customer satisfaction for products and services. We would segment these results by customer groups, as appropriate.
- Trends and current levels in major adverse indicators. Adverse indicators include complaints, claims, refunds, recalls, returns, repeat services, litigation, replacements, downgrades, repairs, warranty costs and warranty work.
- Comparison of customer satisfaction results. We should see if such comparisons can be made with principal competitors in the company's key markets, industry averages, industry leaders and world leaders.

5. *Approach to awards and surveys.* We should examine the details of surveys, competitive awards, recognition and ratings by independent organisations. In so doing we will see how they are organised.
6. *Measuring trends in business results.* We should be looking for trends in gaining or losing customers and in customer and customer account retention. Examine gains and losses of customers, including those gained from or lost to competitors in customer groups or market segments, as appropriate.

   We should also examine trends in gaining and losing market share relative to major competitors, domestic and foreign, and see the reasons for significant changes in quality comparisons and quality trends.

Packaging International
How they measure customer satisfaction

We determine customer satisfaction through personal contacts, the third party customer satisfaction surveys and our Total Quality Fitness Reviews.

1. Our businesses are defined by product, geographic region (United States, Europe, Far East, Latin America) and market. We organise

market segments within each business around End-Use applications, which are characterised by similarities in customers, product requirements and distribution channels. We currently serve over 40 major market segments. Market segments are also defined by customer groups with similar processing capabilities.

Through personal contacts, our Marketing and Technical people provide information on how customers in each market segment think we are doing. Our customer surveys and Total Quality Fitness Reviews provide quantifiable information which helps us verify this feedback. Survey results are grouped by product, key market segment, function in the customer's organisation (RD&E, Purchasing) and by 'sales' or 'strategic customers'. Our customer satisfaction requirements are as follows:

- Product Quality.
- On-Time Delivery.
- Ease of Access.
- Price.
- Knowledge of Associates.

2. Our Customer satisfaction surveys assess what our customers value in a supplier. They identify product quality, marketing support, customer service and business effectiveness issues where improvements would increase customer satisfaction, and determine how our customers compare us with our competitors.

We interview key customer decision makers within the various functions (e.g., Research & Development, Purchasing and Business managers) who are knowledgeable about the use of our product in their operation. Because of their positions, their responses correlate directly to anticipated future market behaviour.

Our businesses use a survey process developed in collaboration with, and conducted by, Customer Surveys Inc. (CSI). Respondents are asked early in the 20-minute interview to identify competitive suppliers. After rating the relative importance of a series of quality factors, customers are asked to rate us and each competitor on a 0–5 scale. (The scale is explained to each respondent, and a word anchor is provided for each number. For example, 5 is excellent, outstanding, the best; 4 is good, better than average). CSI uses retired business executives, who are at ease talking with our external customers. The customers' narrative comments, including their views of our strengths and weaknesses, are documented for our use.

Objectivity is maintained because a third-party firm conducts the survey, the customer remain anonymous of customer, and the interviewers are retired business executives. The design of the survey ensures validity because the consultants have incorporated validation questions throughout the survey. After the results have been tabulated, answers to the questions are compared to assure validity.

Since we began customer satisfaction surveys in 1989, we have completed 24 surveys, interviewing over 1,600 customers, including customers in Korea and Europe. Each business conducts the survey annually. Electrical experimented with quarterly surveys; however, because customers reported this approach was too time-consuming, they now survey annually.

Businesses also use interviews with customers during the Total Quality Fitness Review process. These reviews are global and include customers outside the United States. Customer input on the Fitness Review and the customer survey showed a strong correlation in 1989 and 1990, so we now rely more on the customer satisfaction survey for customer input.

We compare customers' satisfaction with our performance versus our competitors.

1. At least twice a year, all businesses conduct an internal Trade Leader Assessment of Product Quality. Technical Marketing representatives ask our customers a series of questions to determine their level of satisfaction on product suitability and consistency.
2. Using customer survey data on in-kind competitors, we compute Indices of Relative Competitive Position for customer satisfaction. One index is the average rating gap between us and the average of all competitors for each quality factor, weighted for relative importance. The second index, used as a benchmark, is the rating gap between us and a 'hypothetical' BEST competitor, created by the best score for each factor, weighted for relative importance. Customers also provide a 'one-shot' overall satisfaction rating of us and our competitors using the 0–5 scale.

Because of the limited number of in-kind competitors, our re-cyclables products businesses use a more generalised comparison in their surveys. Their customers compare us with other suppliers in the areas of product, customer service, market representative and general business.

Our businesses use customer feedback and their experience to evaluate the survey process and recommend improvements. Business leaders review recommendations from the survey teams and make improvements before the survey is rerun. We annually upgrade our questions to improve clarity, understandability and explicitness. We continue to revise our list of survey participants so we get the information we need.

We moved away from a quarterly frequency to an annual cycle based on customer feedback. Electrical upgraded its survey to use 'paired comparisons' of importance and satisfaction to provide greater accuracy than the 0–5 scale.

Market teams use a variety of approaches to integrate survey feedback with other customer inputs. Comparisons are cross-referenced with information from our direct personal contacts with customers. Food Packaging confirmed the assessment accuracy of its marketing personnel by including several of them as respondents to the customer satisfaction survey. Their responses closely matched the customers in both relative importance and satisfaction levels.

Customer satisfaction results

Overall, we have maintained a consistently high level of customer satisfaction in the areas important to our customers. The sequence of charts in Figure 3.10 indicates our four-year performance against the satisfaction factors included in the 1991 survey.

Leadership reviewed the 1991 survey results and identified responsiveness and customer relationships as opportunities for improvement. Programs were initiated in 1992 to improve these areas. In 1992, customers reported improvements in customer partnerships, responsiveness, understanding of customer requirements and sales representatives. These improvements are also reflected in our competitive comparison.

- Industrial Film received generally outstanding ratings on satisfaction factors but recognised customer relationships as a key area needing improvement. Electrical customer ratings show the need for improvement in on-time delivery and new product development.
- Construction received excellent satisfaction ratings on most factors with significant improvement noted in product quality, understanding customer requirements and responsiveness – all three areas of emphasis in 1991 and the goal of several improvement projects.
- Electrical Packaging showed a strong improvement in satisfaction in 1991. However, our customer satisfaction ratings in 1992 showed a decline in customer service – this is primarily related to an oversold condition overseas which is being addressed by capacity expansion.
- Our re-cyclables customers were significantly more satisfied with product quality.

Figure 3.10

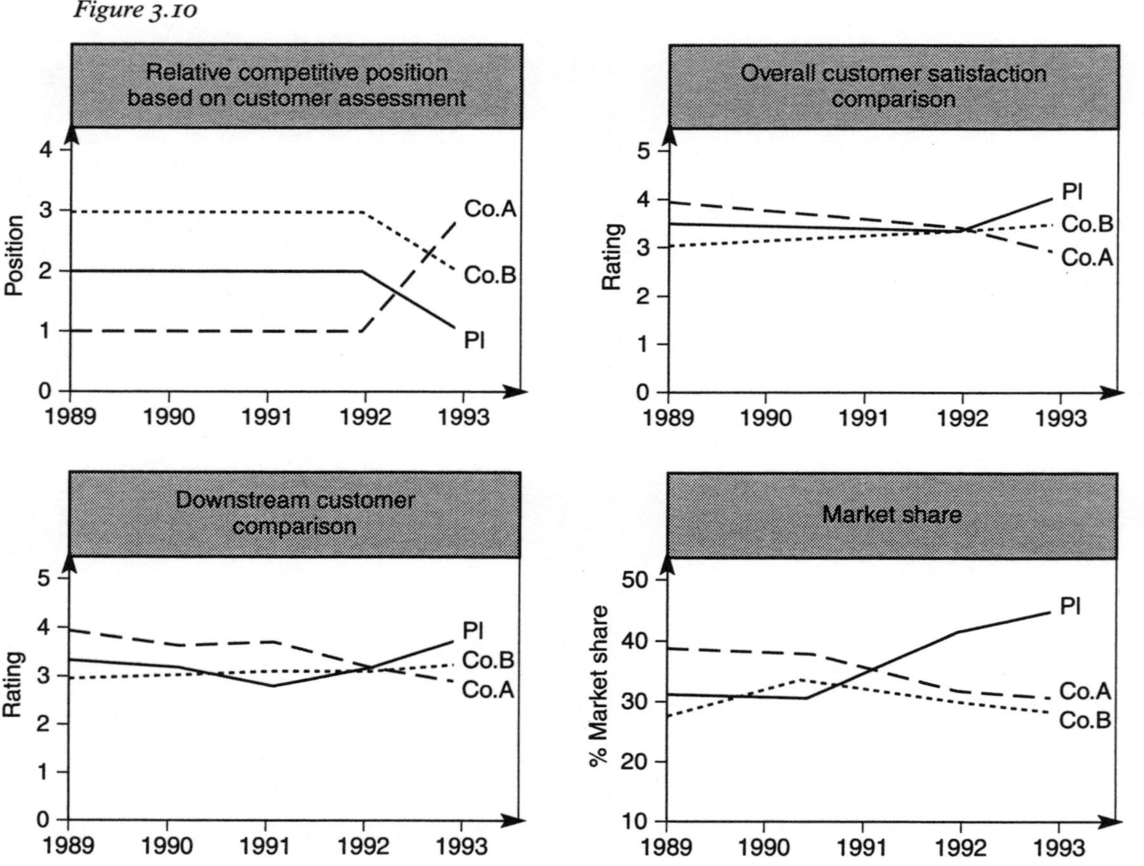
Relative competitive position based on customer assessment
Position
4
3
2
1
0
1989
1990
1991
1992
1993
Co.A
Co.B
PI
Overall customer satisfaction comparison
Rating
5
4
3
2
1
0
1989
1990
1991
1992
1993
PI
Co.B
Co.A
Downstream customer comparison
Rating
5
4
3
2
1
0
1989
1990
1991
1992
1993
PI
Co.B
Co.A
Market share
% Market share
50
40
30
20
10
1989
1990
1991
1992
1993
PI
Co.A
Co.B

Each of our specialty products businesses asked customers to rate our year-to-year progress in overall performance in the areas of products, service, marketing representative and general business. Ninety-four per cent of the customers who rated us believe we are performing better than, or the same as, we were last year.

Our customer dissatisfaction indicators support findings that our customers are satisfied with our products and services.

The number of complaints (Problem Reports) per million pounds shipped is extremely low.

Our claims and our returns are also small.

The packaging businesses enjoy a competitive advantage in customer satisfaction. Our customers compared us with competing suppliers. They rated us higher than the average of all our competitors and comparable to the best-rated competitor in both 1991 and 1992.

For the index of Relative Competitive Position, we had the advantage versus the average of all competitors. (An index of +1.0 means we scored an average one full rating scale unit higher than competition for each of the satisfaction factors.) We also compare our performance against a benchmark, which is a composite competitor credited with the 'best' ratings for each factor. In other words, our benchmark is a standard beyond any of our competitors.

Industrial also surveyed downstream customers in the industrial film industry. Our rating was higher than the best of the competitors in each of the factors.

We maintain long-term relationships with our strategic customers. Our businesses use sales history data to track sales by customers and by market segments quarterly. Given the nature of our businesses, analysis of trends in losing customers to competitors is not very insightful. For example, our Construction business sells to 95 per cent of the existing plants – the number is decreasing as plants go out of business or companies merge. Strong end-use preference and performance warranties drive the majority of retailers to carry our products, which in turn exerts pressure on the plants.

Our businesses are industry leaders, as demonstrated by our large market share. We have increased our market share during the past four years. Using data published by the Film Economic Bureau, an industry-supported association, we track market share for these businesses monthly. However, we do not view market share as the only indicator of customer satisfaction. Our businesses use these data and trends to better understand competitors' tactics, strategies and intent regarding markets and capacity utilisation.

Changes in market share of businesses do not surprise us; they usually reflect protracted negotiations for major programs in the industry or competitive consolidations.

We have developed unique long-term 'value' contracts where Quality improvements are shared with our customers. These aggressive partnerships assure future market share and growth.

Our re-cyclables business has few, if any, in-kind competitors. We generally measure their growth in new applications or substitution rates for functional competition. Where we have in-kind competition, we are the leading supplier, and we enjoy the largest market share.

In this chapter, we have introduced the concept of benchmarking at the process level and the five macro processes which make up the customer service process as a whole, as defined by the Malcolm Baldridge and European Quality Award frameworks. These five subdivided into a total of 27 individual processes, and it is probably worth listing them here as a reference.

Understanding customers' needs

1. Understanding near and long term Customer requirements
2. Projecting future Customer requirements and expectations
3. Determining Customer requirements

Managing customer relationships

4. Identifying key requirements
5. Setting service standards
6. Providing Customer accessibility
7. Stimulating feedback
8. Improving relationships
9. Establishing Commitments
10. Evaluation and improvement

Delivering service through people

11. Providing technology support
12. Stimulating employee involvement
13. Getting feedback
14. Allocating reward and recognition
15. Training
16. Identifying key indicators of well-being

Managing dissatisfaction

17. Handling lost orders/customers
18. Complaint feedback
19. Resolving the complaint
20. Establishing the root cause
21. Improving the complaint process

Measuring customer satisfaction

22. Mechanisms for segmenting
23. Measuring satisfaction relative to competitors
24. Assessing satisfaction with warranty
25. Measuring trends in satisfaction
26. Approach to Awards & Surveys
27. Measuring trends in business results

On reading this chapter you should ask the following questions of your enterprise:

1. Do I take my customers' requirements for granted?
2. Have I ever been surprised by their choice of products and services from competitors?
3. Has my offer stayed roughly the same for the last five years?
4. Do we spend enough time with our customers?
5. Would employees dream of calling a senior manager at home?

6. Do we have difficulty retaining good people to do demanding frontline duties?
7. Do I have difficulty in knowing if our customers are really satisfied?
8. Are satisfaction indicators ever discussed at executive meetings?
9. Do we believe our competitors achieve lower overall satisfaction ratings than us?
10. Has our market share been declining over the last five years?

Results

- *Yes* to more than 7 questions and your customer management processes are in serious need of review.
- *Yes* to between 7 and 3 questions and you are on the way to best practice.
- *Yes* to less than 3 questions and you are already there.

4

MEASUREMENT AND ANALYSIS

In this chapter we discuss:

- Measurement of the process benchmarks.
- Analysis of the findings.
- Linking statistical benchmarks to customer strategy.
- Techniques for data gathering.

MEASUREMENT OF THE PROCESS BENCHMARKS

In the previous chapter we covered the scope of process benchmarking, and here we will look at how to carry out the assessment.

Each process in an organisation is evaluated according to how well and how many of the best practice steps it follows, and the evaluation is carried out for these three areas:

- The approach.
- The deployment.
- The results.

In the evaluation, we are trying to assess how well the organisation sets about serving its customers (*the approach*), how well it executes the approach (*the deployment*) and whether there is evidence in the form of business results to justify those actions (*the results*).

The approach

By approach, we mean the methods the company uses to achieve the requirements we defined earlier. In order to evaluate the approaches we ask one or more of the following questions:

- What is the appropriateness of the methods, tools and techniques of the requirements?
- How effective are the methods, tools and techniques?
- To what degree is the approach systematic, integrated and consistently applied?
- To what degree is the approach based upon effective evaluation and improvement cycles?
- To what degree is the approach based upon quantitative information that is objective and reliable?
- To what degree is the approach prevention-based?
- Are there indicators of unique and innovative approaches, including significant and effective new adaptations of tools and techniques used in other applications or types of business?

The deployment

By deployment, we mean the extent to which the approaches have been applied to all the relevant areas and activities within each of the processes which are to be benchmarked. To assess this we ask the following questions, in each case to do with how well the approach has been applied in practice:

- Has there been an appropriate and effective application of the stated approach by all work units to all processes and activities?
- Has there been an appropriate and effective application of the stated approach to all product and service features?
- Has there been an appropriate and effective application of the stated approach to all transactions and interactions with customers, suppliers of goods and services and the public?

The results

By results, we mean the outcomes and effects of applying the processes. Here, we would ask these questions:

- What are the performance levels?
- What are the quality and performance levels relative to appropriate comparisons and/or benchmarks?
- At what rate has performance improved?
- What is the breadth and importance of the performance improvements?
- Has there been a demonstration of sustained improvement or sustained high-level performance?

Figure 4.1 shows the scoring criteria used. Typically, an organisation that has taken on board only a few of the characteristics of best practice, and implemented them in a pilot within a small part of the organisation, would score poorly. By contrast, an organisation which exhibits extensive use of best practice and has displayed it extensively throughout and can identify good improvements in its business results will score highly.

When we score an organisation, we should ensure consistency, and to do so we recommend two or more scoring assessors. We must bear in mind that the scores are only a guide for comparisons. The real power behind this technique lies in identifying the strengths and weaknesses of the organisation and where it could do things better.

In Figure 4.2 the scoring profile we illustrate the output of an evaluation of a single process. You will appreciate that scoring can be useful in providing a quick view of how your organisation compares with best practice.

For example, your company may have a good tradition of strong customer relationships and therefore will exhibit all the good aspects of that particular process. But on the other hand, the company might

SCORE	APPROACH/DEPLOYMENT
0%	■ No systematic approach evident; anecdotal information.
10% to 30%	■ Beginning of a systematic approach to the primary purpose of the item. ■ Early stages of a transition from reacting to problems to a general improvement orientation. ■ Major gaps exist in deployment that would inhibit progress in achieving the primary purposes of the item.
40% to 60%	■ A sound, systematic approach, responsive to the primary purpose of the item. ■ A fact-based improvement process in place in key areas; more emphasis is placed on improvement than on reaction to problems. ■ No major gaps in deployment, though some areas or work units may be in very early stages of deployment.
70% to 90%	■ A sound, systematic approach, responsive to the primary purposes of the item. ■ A fact-based improvement process is a key management tool; clear evidence of refinement and improved integration as a result of improvement cycles and analysis. ■ Approach is well-deployed, with no major gaps; deployment may vary in some areas or work units.
100%	■ A sound, systematic approach, fully responsive to all the requirements of the item. ■ A very strong, fact-based improvement process is a key management tool; strong refinement and integration – backed by excellent analysis. ■ Approach is fully deployed without any significant weaknesses or gaps in any areas or work units.

SCORE	RESULTS
0%	■ No results or poor results in areas reported.
10% to 30%	■ Early stages of developing trends; some improvements and/or early good performance levels in a few areas. ■ Results not reported for many to most areas of importance to the applicant's key business requirements.
40% to 60%	■ Improvement trends and/or good performance levels reported for many to most areas of importance to the applicant's key business requirements. ■ No pattern of adverse trends and/or poor performance levels in areas of importance to the applicant's key business requirements. ■ Some trends and/or current performance levels – evaluated against relevant comparisons and/or benchmarks – show areas of strength and/or good to very good relative performance levels.
70% to 90%	■ Current performance is good to excellent in most areas of importance to the applicant's key business requirements. ■ Most improvement trends and/or performance levels are sustained. ■ Many to most trends and/or current performance levels – evaluated against relevant comparisons and/or benchmarks – show areas of leadership and very good relative performance levels.
100%	■ Current performance is excellent in most areas of importance to the applicant's key business requirements. ■ Excellent improvement trends and/or sustained excellent performance levels in most areas. ■ Strong evidence of industry and benchmark leadership demonstrated in many areas.

Figure 4.1 Best practice sharing guidelines as used in the EQA.

Figure 4.2 Summary scores of the process benchmarks. Scores are only an approximate measure of how well your organisation goes about customer management in relation to best practice and to your competitors. They give you a means of measuring the success of process improvement programmes.

lag well behind in its effectiveness in managing dissatisfaction and the way it sets about understanding customers. Consequently, these would be the two processes for review if you had decided it was time to do a better job of serving customers. The most urgent of the two would be 'managing satisfaction' because that is where your own organisation lags well behind the average for your sector.

ANALYSIS OF THE FINDINGS

Let's take the example once again of Packaging International and analyse its performance against the first macro process, which you may recall from chapter 3 is *Understanding customer needs.*

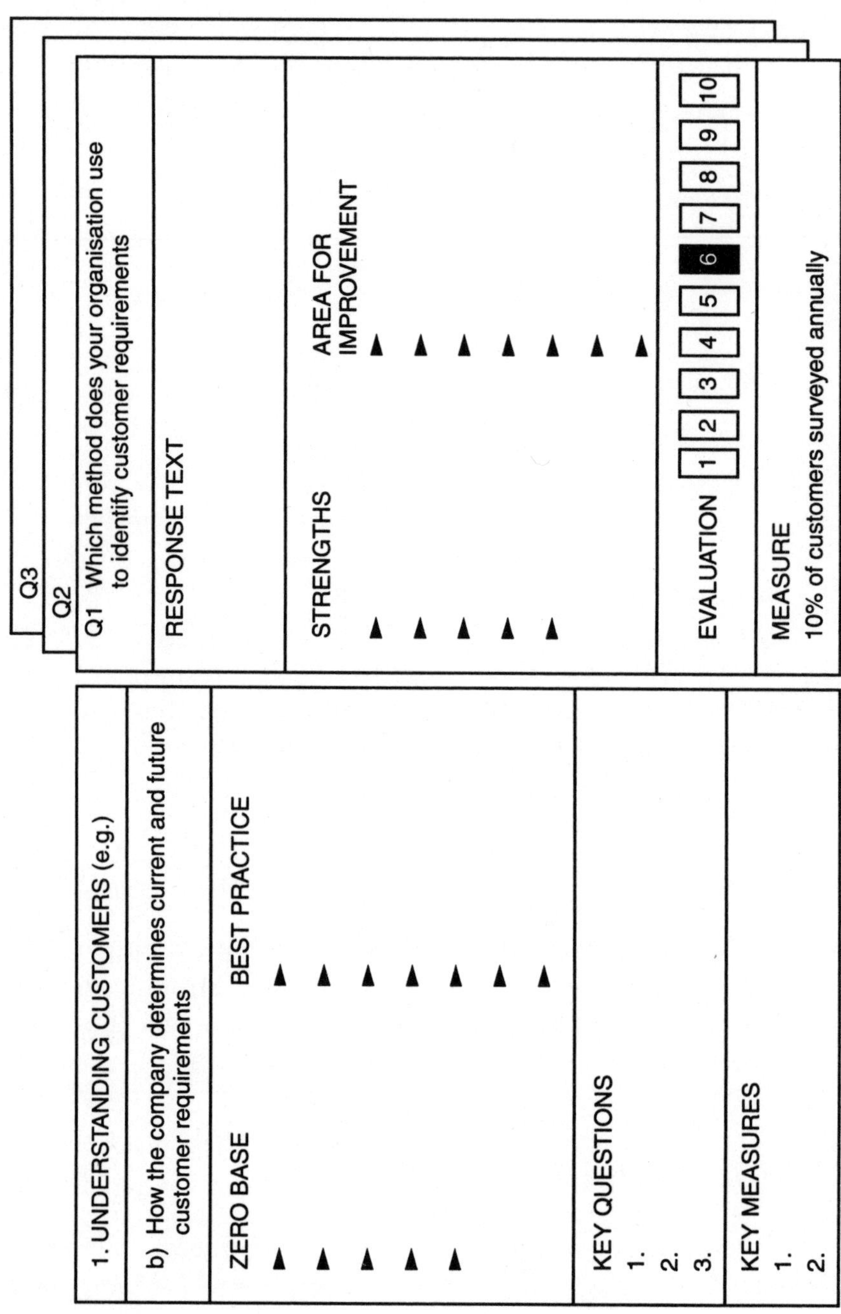
1. UNDERSTANDING CUSTOMERS (e.g.)
b) How the company determines current and future customer requirements
ZERO BASE
BEST PRACTICE
KEY QUESTIONS
1.
2.
3.
KEY MEASURES
1.
2.
Q3
Q2
Q1 Which method does your organisation use to identify customer requirements
RESPONSE TEXT
STRENGTHS
AREA FOR IMPROVEMENT
EVALUATION
1
2
3
4
5
6
7
8
9
10
MEASURE
10% of customers surveyed annually

Figure 4.2(a)

The key assessment points

These are:

- How does PI collect and analyse the variety of data concerning markets?
- How appropriately have their markets been segmented?
- When and how does PI use data generated by independent market researchers to supplement and validate their own research?

The overall purpose is to obtain data that indicates exactly what customers of Packaging International really want now.

The evidence which would demonstrate success

This would be as follows:

- PI has a systematic process of collecting and analysing a variety of market data.
- The documentation of market needs must have been included as an important element in their strategic plans.
- There are in place effective methods of gathering customer input for the analysis process.

The current strengths of PI

Knowing their current strengths will enable PI to improve significantly appropriate customer service processes. They are as follows:

- Individuals within the organisation have a detailed knowledge of current customers which is supported by strong individual informal contacts.
- Competitive and industry trends have been thoroughly understood and used in proposing and performing work with customers.
- Packaging International is recognised as a major player in the packaging market.
- There is a systematic approach for assessing market and customer requirements.
- There is evidence of a long-term strategic plan stating current market position, desired position and methodology to reach specific, quantifiable goals.

- The organisation aims to provide what customers want now, and to use market knowledge to predict future requirements and develop them into products ensuring leadership in its chosen markets.

The areas for improvement

These will provide the initial input for improving the approach and the deployment of customer service processes to enable PI to improve performance significantly. They are as follows:

- The segmentation of markets and customers is limited.
- Customer complaints are handled reactively and the information is not systematically cross-referenced as part of determining customer needs.
- Comparisons with competitive offerings could be improved and there appear to be no well-established means of accepting or rejecting things which competitors did better.

Assessment score and profile

Taking everything into consideration, Packaging International was assessed with a creditable score of 60 per cent. It had an approach which placed significantly more emphasis on problem prevention than reaction to problems and that the macro process of *Understanding customer needs* was fairly well deployed in the business with no major gaps and relatively few weaknesses.

Your own performance

Here you might take the opportunity of assessing your own organisation for the same process, and discover to your disappointment that the score was only 25 per cent. This would represent a significant gap in the process under review, and you might conclude that addressing issues such as these could help close the gap:

- Third-party customer surveys need to be reviewed by the entire management team, not just by marketing.
- Trade show participation should in future incorporate customer feedback rather than product promotions.
- Technical and R&D teams should meet customers on a more frequent basis.

- There is a need to work more creatively at determining future customer needs. Some of PI's ideas of working with focus groups and academic institutions could be adopted.

In this analysis you will have seen that for a single process (and you may recall from chapter 3 that there are a total of 27 in the suggested framework), the organisation has generated at least four fundamental improvement ideas. It is not unusual to end up with improvement opportunities which exceed 100.

Just as with most companies facing the difficulties of change, the real challenge is in harnessing all these good ideas into an integrated plan for improvement. We shall discuss this in chapter 5.

LINKING STATISTICAL BENCHMARKS TO CUSTOMER STRATEGY

General comments

To avoid needless effort and expenditure gathering data for benchmarks we need to link our benchmarking data to our customer strategy. Any other statistics which fall outside the framework of these linkages should be discouraged. Data overload (which often leads to a nasty case of analysis paralysis) can be just as confusing as the lack of it.

Figure 4.3 charts the links from the statement of a customer strategy through the characteristics of the processes involved, then on to the process enablers and finally to the statistical benchmarks.

In this example we consider two organisations that have elected to make as their focus the 'voice of the customer' – i.e. '*Everything we do is driven by you*' from Ford, and '*The listening bank*' from Midland, a UK clearing bank. Both these organisations have set the objective that this is how they wish to be famous in the minds of their customers. The processes are the means by which they hope to achieve this customer service strategy.

To achieve a strategy such as this, it almost goes without saying that they must enable easy customer communication. Thus, if a customer wishes to pass comment on the product or service, then the means to do so should be simple and not involve the need to cut through a mountain of bureaucracy.

Figure 4.3 An illustration of linking statistical benchmarks to customer service strategy.

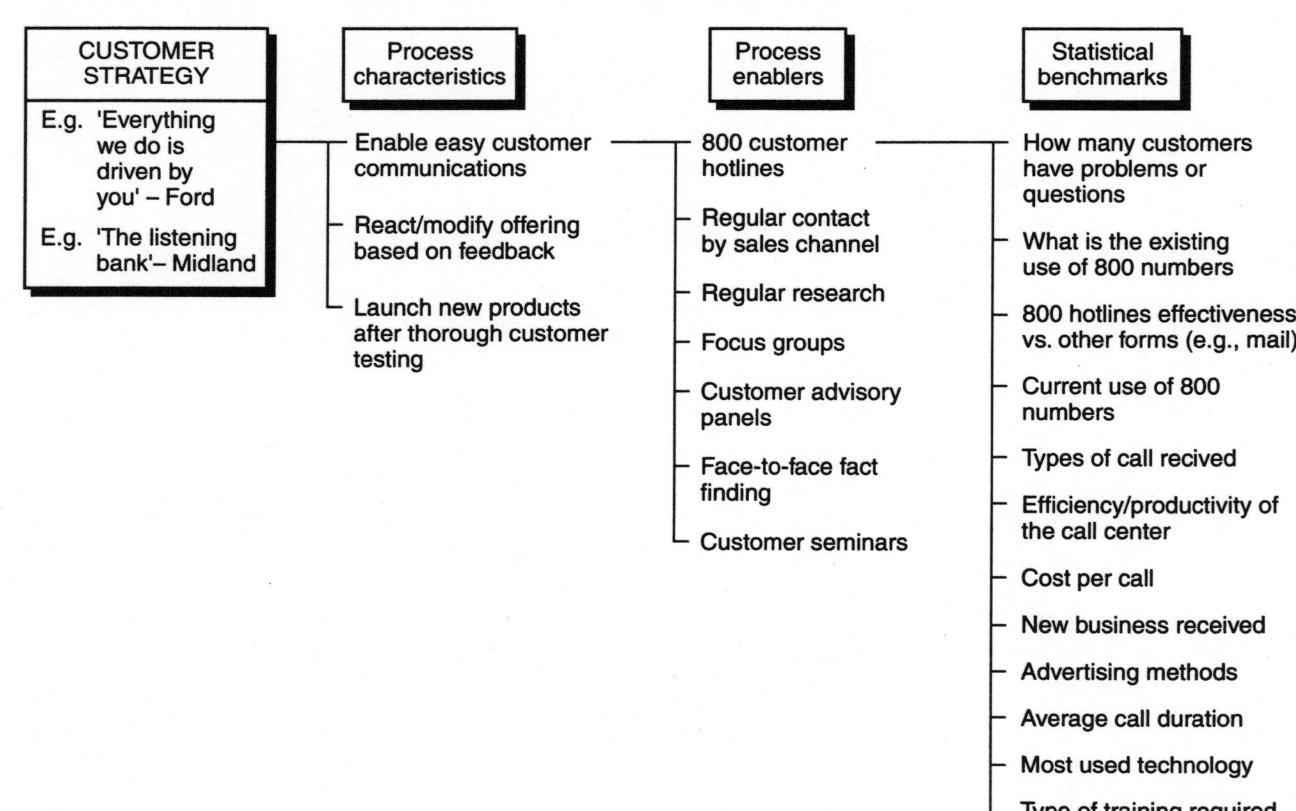

In Japan, train commuters are encouraged to pass on their comments about their train service via green kiosks placed at every station. Most hotels ask you to fill out comment forms placed in your room and some organisations even incentivise customers to provide this form of feedback. This one single process of introducing easy communications may have a number of process enablers. As an example, Figure 4.3 lists potential enablers as:

- 800 customer hot lines
- Regular sales calling
- Regular research
- Focus groups
- Customer advisory panels
- Face-to-face fact finding sessions
- Customer seminars.

Statistical benchmarks

In order to define the statistical benchmarks we will first need to carry out the following:

- Define the offering.
- Monitor the offering.
- Modify the service offering.

Define the offering

How should each process enabler be designed and integrated into the overall service offering? Clearly most service offerings have costs

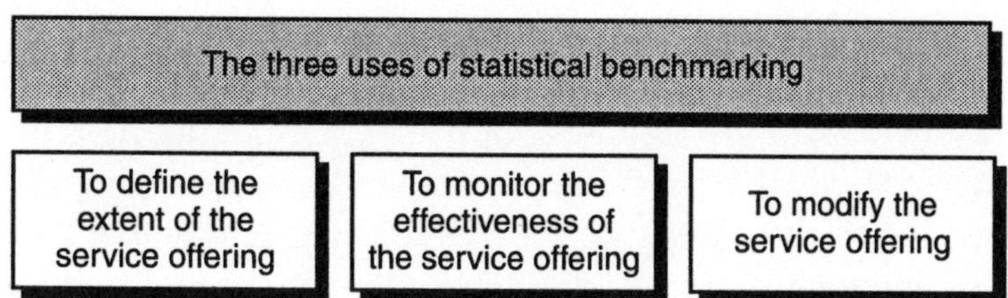

Figure 4.4 The three uses of statistical benchmarks.

associated with them and we need to use benchmarking to identify the extent of that investment to enable our service to provide competitive advantage.

Assuming that most healthy competition never stands still, today's competitive advantage will soon be eroded unless the leader continues to improve its own service performance ahead of the competition. While Marks & Spencer were once renowned for their no-quibble replacement guarantee, today most major retailers offer similar guarantees. Benchmarking can therefore be a useful means of defining the initial service offering at a level comfortably ahead of the competition and as we will see below, also as a means of staying ahead.

Monitor the offering

Having defined the offering, we need to monitor our customers' perceptions of the service levels we have defined and compare them against actual measures of operational performance.

For example, while the railway company may achieve seemingly impressive targets of trains arriving at their destination 98 per cent of the time within five minutes of the published timetable, passengers appear to hold a less favourable view of the timeliness of their trains. We might ask, 'How does the company's performance compare with its competitors?' We should examine this both in terms of customer perceptions and actual performance compared with its competitors. The latter benchmarks are more difficult to obtain.

Modify the service offering.

If we fail to achieve the planned service levels, we need to examine ways in which we can improve performance. On the other hand, if we are already achieving or even exceeding our targets, but customer perceptions remain worryingly unaltered, we need to review whether we have set the correct service levels, or if we are using the right benchmarks, or if there are other factors which previously we did not foresee.

Returning to the railway company's 'timeliness', the gap between the company's actual performance and their customers' perceptions may be due to the organisation measuring train arrivals rather than passenger miles. Timeliness in respect of passenger miles might be a more accurate reflection of how the customers are actually affected. Or perhaps it is the case that on the few occasions when passengers are delayed, the lack of information about the delay causes unforgettable distress which is not corrected by the passage of time.

Perhaps modifying the service offering by providing more information and passenger assistance when delays occur would have a better affect on improving customer perceptions than improving timeliness from 98 per cent to 99 per cent.

Benchmarks to define the offer

Let us look at an example of the use of statistical benchmarks to help in defining a new service offering.

Our service strategy in Figure 4.3 describes the organisation as being customer led. One of the characteristics to achieve this is assumed to be the provision of easy customer communications, and this is enabled by a number of processes, one of which is the use of 800 customer hotlines to channel comments and complaints about the service received.

The discussion below describes how we might go about defining the hotline service by benchmarking existing hotlines offered by other companies and the attitudes of customers towards the service. Notice how the use of both sector and cross-sector comparisons are used in defining this service.

- *What is the incidence of customers having problems or queries regarding their purchase?*
  This benchmark sets the scene regarding the extent of demand for customers to get in touch. A low demand would indicate that the service is not necessary, while a high demand would give it a high degree of priority. The benchmarks in Figure 4.5 show that there is such a demand. In Auto Sales, the target sector we have chosen for this example, the fact is that 35–50 per cent of customers need to get in touch within three months of the purchase.
- *What is the existing and potential use of 800 numbers by customers?*
  Clearly, if there is a low incidence of use or resistance to use this method of communication, then we may want to wait till customers are ready to use it. The target sector for these benchmarked companies needs to be wider than our own as we are trying to

establish customer attitudes. The same customers buy products and services from a variety of companies in different sectors.

The benchmarks show a high degree of desire for hotlines by customers, and a good take-up rate in at least one segment. Our target segment indicates very low current use, signifying an opportunity to introduce such a service (Figure 4.6).

- *How effective are hotlines versus other forms of communication?* We need to establish whether the same ambition of providing easy

Segment	% with Questions/problems	Time since purchase
Automotive sales/service	35% - 50%	1 month
Computers	40% - 75%	3 months
Office equipment	20% - 50%	3 months
White goods	10% - 20%	6 months

Figure 4.5 Incidence of problems and time since purchase.

Segment	% Current use	% Likely to use
Automotive sales/service	10%	70%
Computers	60%	90%
Office equipment	20%	70%
White goods	15%	65%

Figure 4.6 The current and desired use of 800 hotlines.

communication for our customers may be achieved by some other means – perhaps mail or freepost.

Here we would poll customers' perceptions irrespective of segment, because the means of communication is a reflection of customer attitude irrespective of, and not related to, any particular industry segment. We should also benchmark real volumes of communications for an organisation which offers all three media.

From the benchmarks we discover that customer preferences show overwhelming support for 800 hotlines (Figure 4.7). However, in reality, the gap is less significant, and this may be due to mechanistic reasons. Customers might not be able to remember or be able easily to find the hotline number when they most need it. And to this we must add the simple fact that putting things down in writing represents a stronger and more auditable channel of communication, so customers may still resort to the written word when they want to complain.

Current trends in the use of 800 numbers

We need to establish if the trend for hotlines is on an increase, so in this benchmark we should look at a number of segments all serving a common customer. Clearly, if the trend is upwards we may have no option but to offer such a service before many of our competitors do.

		800 Hotline	Freepost	Traditional mail
% Customers showing preference to use a medium		75%	35%	10%
Actual volumes	Airline	40%	30%	30%
	Utility	50%	20%	30%

Figure 4.7 Comparing of different media of communication.

	% Companies using 800 hotline		
	1990	1993	1996 (estimate)
Automotive sales/service	0%	20%	80%
Utilities	10%	30%	70%
Financial services	15%	40%	60%
Retail white goods	10%	20%	50%
Computers	20%	55%	90%
Office equipment	30%	60%	80%

Figure 4.8 Trends in the use of hotlines.

Indeed, benchmarks show that 80 per cent of companies in our target sector intend offering 800 number hotlines (Figure 4.8). In fact, in most sectors in the future we would expect to see customer hotlines on offer. Before long customers will begin to take these services for granted and we will need to find an alternative strategy for making communications easy and maintaining a differential against our competitors.

What are the types of transaction handled on hotlines?

We want to establish the types of communications handled on hotlines, as this will determine the training and resourcing requirements for the contact centre. A consolidated view of all existing companies using hotlines would be one set of data compared with our own target sector. Finally, comparisons within our own existing organisation's current arrangements should be made. This is illustrated in Figure 4.9.

	% Calls from customers		
	Complaints	Enquiries	New sales
All industry segments	35%	55%	10%
Automotive sales/service	50%	35%	15%
Our current organisation (No advertised hotline)	70%	30%	0%

Figure 4.9 Why do people use hotlines?

The benchmarks reveal that our in our target sector, hotline communications are especially dominated by complaints (50 per cent) followed by transaction enquiries at (35 per cent). Interestingly a significant 15 per cent of all those transactions were for new business compared with a non-existent percentage of similar enquiries for our existing organisation. This information will be useful later in cost justifying an investment in the 800 hotline facility.

Analysis of new business received

We may wish to carry out an analysis of new business attributable to the hotline, as the volume and profitability of this incremental revenue might then support our overall customer strategy. Clearly, these

	% Average increase in new business post 800 introduction	Average sale value	Average margins	ROI
Automotive sales/service	20%	$270	$75	22%
Last campaign	2% (After launch)	$7,000	$250	14%

Figure 4.10 Analysis of new business post hotline introduction.

benchmarks need to be segment-specific and this presents us with a problem of data collection, for which we would probably have to rely on the telecommunications company providing the service.

Should we be successful in obtaining the data, we will possess valuable information. We could compare the new business results from the hotline to those from the latest marketing campaign where a similar value had been invested. We might discover that the return on investment appears to be higher, and this discovery alone would be sufficient to satisfy most corporate guidelines and thereby justify the strategy (Figure 4.10).

What levels of productivity can we expect from the call centre?

In planning the design of the call centre or examining the productivity of our existing call centre we need to compare other organisations' experience. Here, we need to look at average call durations and sector-specific benchmarks. We are able to capture a wide scope of practice by including all sectors.

The benchmarks obtained tell us that our target sector under-performs with regard to overall productivity and under-pays its telephone representatives (Figure 4.11).

	Average call length	After call	Average salary	Calls per rep
All industries	7 minutes	80 sec	$18,500	55
Automotive sales/service	6.5 minutes	70 sec	$14,000	40

Figure 4.11 Productivity of representatives.

What advertising methods are used to promote hotlines?

Here we take into account the most commonly used means of promoting hotlines and use this analysis to design our own advertising programme.

What technology is being used by call centres?

Again, these benchmarks will be useful in helping design the infrastructure of the call centre. The data does not need to be sector-specific. We find from the benchmarks that automated call distribution (ACD) technology is used most frequently, along with voice processing technology. Most companies have to write customised software to supplement the off-the-shelf telecommunications technology (Figure 4.12)

	% Using ACD	% Using voise processing	Average answer speed	Use of custom software
All industries	60%	65%	15 sec	70%

Figure 4.12 Use of technology.

What training do we need to provide?

These benchmarks will be useful in establishing the training programme necessary for staff at the call centre. We find that product and service education occupies the lion's share of the training time (Figure 4.13).

Training in:	Average time of training
Telephone techniques	8 hours
Operating policies	7 hours
Product/service education	20 hours
Dealing with hostility/negotiating	5 hours
System procedures	7 hours
Writing replies	4 hours
Average weeks training	1.5 weeks

Figure 4.13 Training provided to representatives.

Are customers satisfied with the hotline services they use?

Although only 10 per cent of customers in the target sector use a hotline service, overall satisfaction with the service is moderately good. Customers report that while they are pleased with the quality of the telephone representatives, considerable improvement can be made to the speed of reaction to the enquiry and the way in which the hotline number is communicated to customers. These are two design features which must be considered before launching the service (Figure 4.14).

Monitoring the offering

Similar benchmarks may be used to monitor the quality of the service hotline once it has become operational. However, we would only benchmark critical elements of the service rather than the extensive data gathering exercise we originally carried out when defining it.

		Auto sales/service	Other
% Customers used service		10%	20%
Overall satisfaction level		60%	75%
Features	Telephone representatives	80%	70%
	Finding the number	30%	45%
	Speed of reaction to call	40%	60%

Figure 4.14 Satisfaction with existing hotline services.

Many companies carry out satisfaction studies, but few conduct those studies in comparison to what competitors offer – which is of course the essence of benchmarking. Customers' views on satisfaction are only of real value when measured in relation to other vendor–consumer relationships. For example, they could report to you that they are 'satisfied' with your speed of response, but with regard to your competitors' response they may be 'delighted'. The former information in isolation may indicate no cause for action, while knowing the latter may make the improvement of the service critically important.

The frequency of the benchmarking activity will depend on the type of service you offer. If customers are making daily buying decisions about your product, then degradation in service levels can very quickly result in lost sales. Benchmarking must therefore be carried out frequently.

Federal Express, whose customers are making daily decisions about parcel services, survey their market monthly. IBM survey their customers quarterly because in their case buying decisions are made less frequently. And major telecommunications providers such as AT&T and BT carry out annual corporate buyer surveys where decisions on purchasing are made every few years.

Modifying the offering

It would be wrong to assume that having once defined the offering, the needs of customers will remain unchanged for the foreseeable future. Witness the speed of change in today's social and commercial environment and you will soon be aware of the danger in this assumption.

At appropriate intervals it will be necessary to check your assumptions with customers by making comparisons with other competitors and, in addition, organisations outside your sector. For example, five years ago customers may have reacted unenthusiastically to the idea of a creche attached to their local cinema. But now, with a change in demographics in the area, more single-parent families and a waning demand in home videos, customers may value the idea of their offspring being cared for while they watch the latest release from Hollywood.

TECHNIQUES FOR DATA GATHERING

Measuring customer perceptions

The accurate capture of customers' perceptions of your products and services can provide one of the greatest sources of competitive advantage. But, as many market researchers have discovered, customers may not always tell you what they really mean or in some cases what they actually want.

Also, in some of today's markets where it is increasingly difficult to differentiate on service because this has never been seriously exploited by companies, the customer may have no idea of the additional features which may enhance the offer. Innovation in the bench marking exercise is important to identify potential features.

The three most important points to realise in measuring perceptions are that the measurement system needs to display:

- simplicity;
- adequacy;
- and consistency.

Figure 4.15 shows how different scales of accuracy may be used to benchmark perceptions.

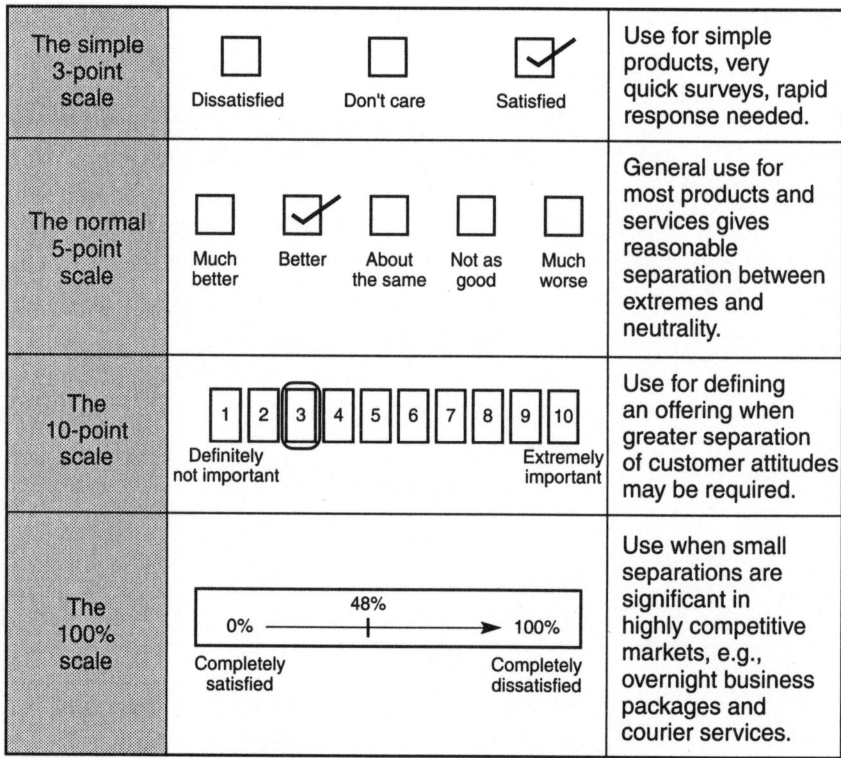

Figure 4.15 Different scales of accuracy should be used depending on the types of benchmarking being conducted. A simple three-point scale is useful, particularly in telephone interviews and where rapid response is required. At the other extreme, a 100 per cent scale helps define accurately customer perceptions where small differences can make a great deal of difference.

Simplicity should manifest itself in the form of expressions which the customer can immediately associate with the service he or she receives. Asking the average consumer who shops at the local hypermarket to rate the convenience of the store layout directly on a scale of 1 to 100 may not be the most effective way of capturing perceptions. Translate the questions to words such as 'delighted', 'extremely important', 'inadequately met' and 'no firm view', and customers can form recognisable frames of reference to convey their perceptions.

With regard to *adequacy*, there are some cases where only small incremental changes to services can alter the field of competition. Here a more extensive means of calibrating perceptions may be preferred, particularly if the buyer is comfortable with numerical forms of evaluation. For example, a buyer of energy services for a local authority may be comfortable with a scoring system which starts at say 0 per cent for complete satisfaction and 100 per cent for complete dissatisfaction.

We are only likely to achieve *consistency* of measurement throughout a customer segment if all benchmarking in the organisation is carried out using the same measurement system. At Motorola, the account managers, field sales force, independent researchers and top management all use the same measurement criteria when visiting or surveying customers. In this way, customer perceptions can be compared meaningfully, and correlated in the assurance that consistent metrics have been used at all levels of measurement.

There has been considerable debate of late on the survey sample used in customer benchmarking studies. Generally, companies only include existing accounts in their customer surveys, and in most consumer research, frequent random sampling is used to remove bias.

However, there is a strong argument that benchmarking criteria should be skewed significantly in favour of customers who have defected to competitors' offerings. The rationale for this is simply that the reasons for the defection are the ultimate call for action, while all other perceptions are subject to interpretation.

If a customer said he quit because your billing procedures were cumbersome and the view is backed up by a good proportion of defectors, then you had better do something about fixing the billing procedure soon or the trickle of defections may soon become a flood.

The argument is doubly persuasive when you consider that customer defections are early indicators of trends in the availability of competing offerings and their attractiveness to customers.

Please rate our proposal against winning bid for the following criteria		Our score (Poor → Excellent)	Winner's score
1	Approach to the work	1 2 3 4 5 6 7 8 9 10	
2	Skills and resources proposed	1 2 3 4 5 6 7 8 9 10	
3	Confidence in the team	1 2 3 4 5 6 7 8 9 10	
4	Previous experience of company/sector	1 2 3 4 5 6 7 8 9 10	
5	Clarity of work programme and deliverables	1 2 3 4 5 6 7 8 9 10	
6	Quality of references	1 2 3 4 5 6 7 8 9 10	
7	Technical content of proposal	1 2 3 4 5 6 7 8 9 10	
8	Diagnosis of the problem	1 2 3 4 5 6 7 8 9 10	
9	Reputation of firm	1 2 3 4 5 6 7 8 9 10	
10	Price	1 2 3 4 5 6 7 8 9 10	

Figure 4.16 Benchmarking lost proposals. Every lost customer is an opportunity to improve your offering. It is important to benchmark competitor wins with your offering and initiate, where necessary, remedial action. This analysis shows a simple 10-point evaluation form which is best completed by the decision maker shortly after the award announcement.

At Price Waterhouse, every time I lose a proposal to a competitor I ask the prospective client to rate my proposal against the winner and hope therefore to gain ideas from that feedback to act upon the next time around. Every lost proposal represents an opportunity for me to learn about my approach to gaining new business, to understand better how the resources might be used, the way the proposal process was handled and the pricing of the bid. But it also tells me a great deal about my competitors and when all the information is used wisely it will help me improve my conversion rate. An example of this feedback analysis is shown in Figure 4.16.

Customer focus groups

Customer focus groups have been used for some time to assess customer perception on a company's existing and future products and services. Although still a relatively new idea in Europe, the technique has been around for some time in North America and some US companies are now reporting an increased resistance from customers to participate in them.

Without doubt they have proved themselves effective in determining product features, segmenting the market, understanding what drives purchase behaviour and identifying satisfiers and dissatisfiers. They are less effective as a means of measuring satisfaction as members of the group tend to influence each other when providing feedback.

Figure 4.17 shows how different measurement techniques have been shown to be effective for a range of benchmarking purposes.

Here are a few tips on constructing a customer focus group:

1. *Representative sample*

For benchmarking studies you should have a representative sample of customers. Choose your sample of invited guests carefully and avoid an overpopulation of customers with whom the account teams feel comfortable. Invite recent defections or known accounts of your competitors.

2. *Offer incentives*

You should consider the idea of offering incentives for those who

		Qualitative customer interviews/ focus groups	Internal focus groups	Quantitative surveys	Conjoint analysis
1	Identifying dominant PRODUCT features	✓			✓
2	Segmentation of SALES market	✓		✓	
3	What drives purchase behaviour?	✓	✓		
4	Identify satisfiers/ dissatifiers	✓	✓		
5	Satisfaction ratings			✓	
6	Company performance ratings			✓	
7	Identify CULTURAL barriers within company	✓	✓		

Figure 4.17 Measurement techniques and their application to benchmarking. Experience shows that techniques need to be applied to the appropriate circumstances. Focus groups, for example, have not been known to be suitable for satisfaction ratings because of the likelihood of group bias.

agree to attend, but take care because incentives can be a turnoff or attract attendance for the wrong reasons. An incentive such as a pleasant dinner in a private room at a well-known restaurant in town can provide the ideal catalyst for attracting participants.

In other instances, customers may welcome an invitation to look behind the scenes within the supplier's organisation. Alternatively, going back stage in a television studio, into the boardroom of a major corporation or a visit to the R&D laboratories of a hi-tech supplier are examples of incentives which may attract participants.

3. *Structured questioning*

Questioning needs to be structured so that you cover comments on all aspects of your service offering. Let's assume your retail service offering is to be 'fast, friendly, safe and clean'. Questions need to cover the speed with which customers can collect their purchase and pay for them, whether staff appear helpful and friendly in their manner and their greeting, whether the entrances, exits and other safety features cause concern, and if the retail area, together with services such as lavatories, appear clean.

4. *Assessments*

Try whenever possible to get customers to give you a standard adjective to describe each feature together with comments. Assessments should be given for each feature before discussion on that feature. As an example you could say, '... Ladies and Gentleman, I would like you to describe the speed of our checkout. Please tick the box which best describes this ...'. You then welcome discussion. By doing this you avoid a particularly vocal participant influencing others in the group.

5. *Invite comments*

Invite comments on competitors after having received your assessments: 'Could you describe each of the following companies for speed of checkout: Company A, Company B, Company C ...?'. You can then ask them to comment on one aspect which a competitor does better. Also ask the participants to nominate one non-competitor which is their most admired company for service. One retailer I know uses airlines to convey an image for comparison purposes.

6. *Assess the service offering*

Finally, ask the participants to assess the importance to them of your service offering. They should score the service features in order of importance. This is intended as a continual check to ensure that the company has the right service offering in order of perceived importance to the customer.

Focus group layout

When designing focus groups, it is important to ensure that management and their frontline teams capture the comments made – in other words 'the voice of the customer'. Views and opinions captured in written notes or tables of data have less impact than face-to-face commentary from individuals talking to the people they deal with.

One of the best ideas I have seen in designing focus groups was introduced to me by Ron Zenke and Chip Bell. In their format, which is best described as a 'staged session', the participants sit in the centre of the room, usually around a table chaired by a facilitator. They are ringed by a representative sample of frontline team members drawn from, say, Sales, Distribution, Engineering and Accounts. The management team sit on the outermost ring.

The customer panel sits in session for between one and two hours, during which time the company's representatives listen in silence. The participants are asked to score cards without influencing each other and open commentary is invited after each attribute has been scored. At the end of the session, the participants leave and are replaced by the frontline team in the inner circle. The team discusses the results based on their own experience, the benchmark cards are reviewed and comments are made on the findings. Team members agree or disagree with the scores and comments. Finally, the team representatives leave the room and their places are taken by the management group who agree on the action plan.

You can appreciate why focus groups are a powerful device in involving a wide cross-section of the service organisation in benchmarking its own offering. Focus groups are illustrated in Figures 4.18(a), (b) and (c).

The mystery customer

The use of anonymous customers specially hired to benchmark service levels is widely used by the retail and leisure industries to compare critical areas of service. Generally, the organisation hires

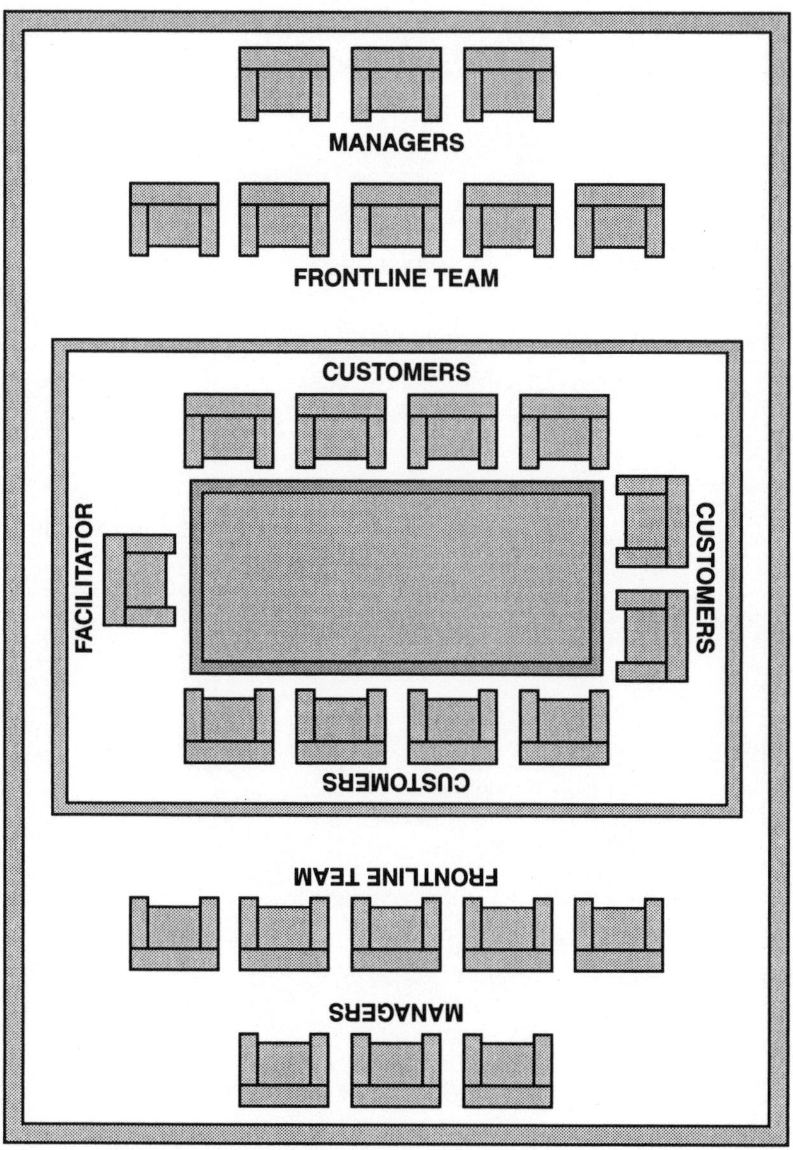

Figure 4.18(a) The focus group in its primary format with customers led by a facilitator, ringed by members of the frontline team and managers. Only customers speak.

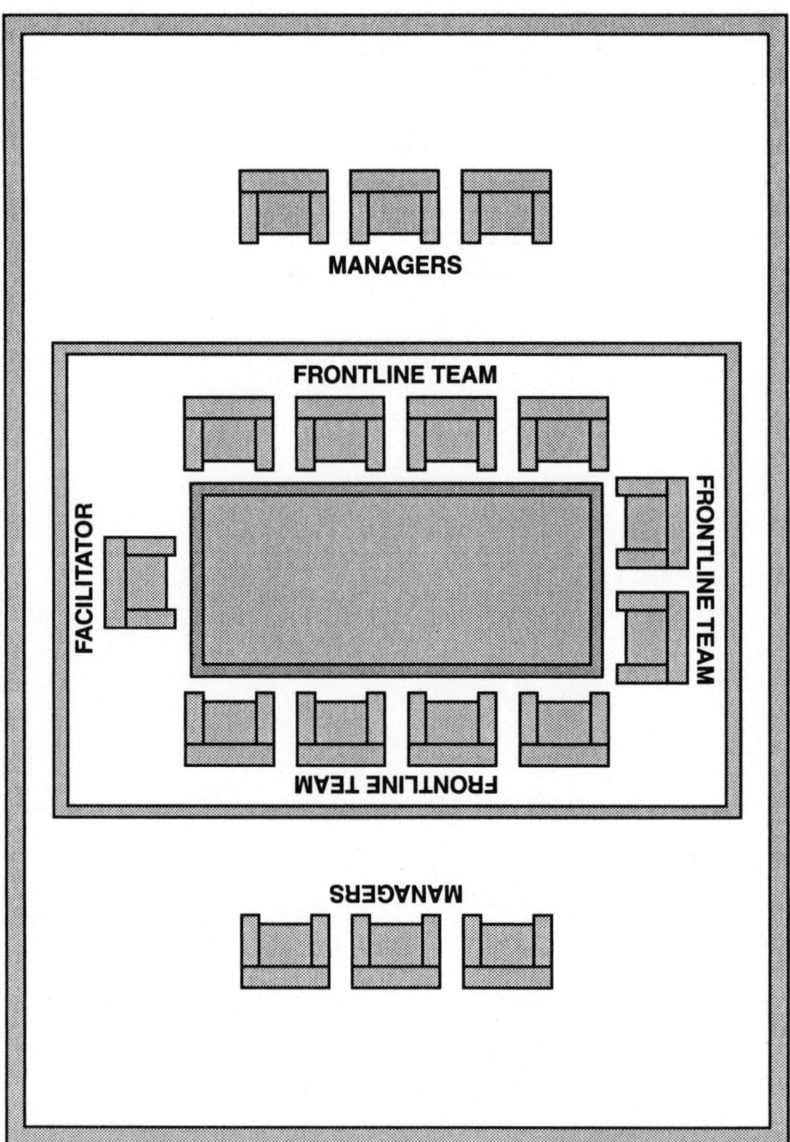

Figure 4.18(b) The focus group in its secondary format with frontline team and managers. Managers listen.

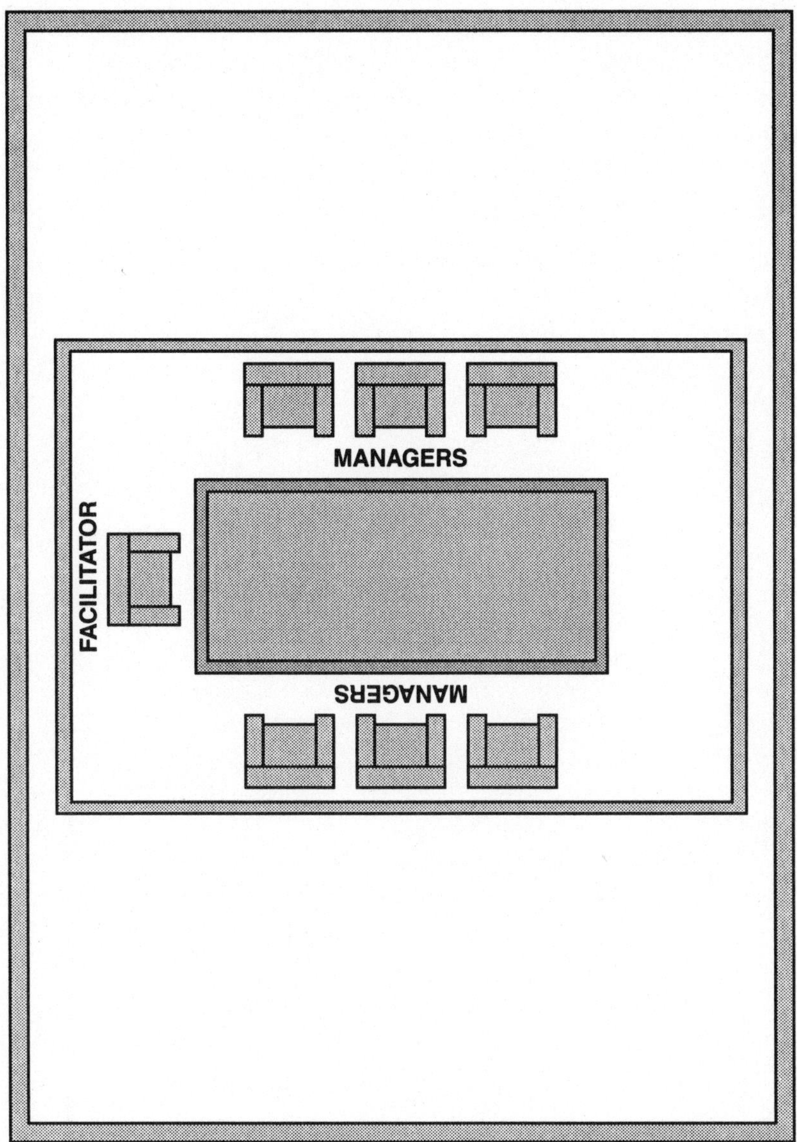

Figure 4.18(c) The group with managers responding to the views expressed earlier.

outsiders to buy goods and experience the entire service without the frontline employees being aware of their 'mystery role'.

The service components are defined to an unambiguous level of detail, as illustrated in Figure 4.19. The 'friendly' characteristics of the offer are defined by a number of detailed behaviours and reactions from staff. For example:

- Did staff at the point of payment greet the customer as he or she walked up to the till?
- After payment by credit card, did the staff member hand back the card and receipt calling the customer by name?
- What was the novelty of the greeting and did the assistant show any interest in the customer?

SERVICE CHARACTERISTICS

FRIENDLY

Level of acknowledgement at first contact:

greeting YES NO novelty of greeting

Level of interest in customer in response to queries:

satifaction with response GOOD POOR

Did staff use name of customer after handing back credit card? YES NO

Farewell exchange inviting customer to patronise again? YES NO

Figure 4.19 Mystery customer assessments of one of the service characteristics. The assessment needs to be defined with the least ambiguity.

- Did the farewell exchange include an invitation to the customer to patronise the establishment again?

Mystery customers are a powerful means of benchmarking the battleground for customers. Access is frequently open to all competitors and the benchmarks measure the reality of the service on offer rather than the publicised intention or strategy employed by the organisation.

Quantitative surveys

Quantitative surveys carried out with a wider cross-section of customers help to monitor satisfaction ratings and compare your organisation with competitors. Exit interviews with customers leaving a retail site is a good point at which to benchmark customer perceptions. Figure 4.20 shows the output from quantitative surveys of customers benchmarked against the service offer.

Service offer	Priority	Our score	Company A	Company B	Comments
Fast	0.4	7 / 2.8	6 / 2.4	8 / 3.2	Company B has better layout
Friendly	0.3	4 / 1.2	6 / 1.8	7 / 2.1	Company B staff always welcome you with a smile
Safe	0.1	5 / 0.5	4 / 0.4	5 / 0.5	No differentiation
Clean	0.2	6 / 1.2	8 / 1.6	8 / 1.6	Both A and B have very clean facilities
Consolidated scores		5.7	6.2	7.4	

Figure 4.20 Quantitative benchmarks of a service offer.

On reading this chapter you should ask the following questions of your own enterprise:

1. Are your best practice processes evenly deployed throughout the organisation?
2. Do the units that exhibit best practice also have correspondingly positive results?
3. Does your benchmarking as it is currently carried out relate to the service proposition?
4. Are benchmarks used to help define or modify your existing offering?
5. Are you using the correct measurement techniques to gather benchmarking data?

You will find answers to these questions in Chapter 4.

5

BENCHMARKING TO ENHANCE SHAREHOLDER VALUE

For many senior managers, shareholder value has become the greatest single objective following concern about the lack of confidence from shareholders. Many companies, once the darlings of the market, have begun to under-perform against the market trend, and in some cases by a significant margin. This concern has led management to begin to put in place strategies which would positively influence share value.

WHAT INFLUENCES SHAREHOLDER VALUE?

In the 1980s, Professor Rappaport suggested a model for assessing shareholder value, and a number of analysts have used it to calculate the theoretical share value of an enterprise. If the calculated value is less than the existing market price, then an analyst would tend to advise clients to sell their stock in the company. Conversely, if the assessed value is higher than the market price, then a 'buy' recommendation would seem appropriate.

A few smart managers soon latched onto the idea that if they could reverse the model and operate the company in a way that could influence the model, they could effectively begin to improve shareholder value. Apart from making the shareholders very happy, it also motivates management and employees who themselves frequently hold stock in the company.

THE VALUE DRIVERS

The Rappaport model is based on seven value drivers. They are as follows:

1. The percentage increase in sales year on year.
2. The operating margins i.e., the difference between costs and income.
3. The value duration – in other words the time over which a product or service costs more to keep on than the revenue it generates.
4. The cost of capital.
5. Working capital including inventory, credit, etc.
6. The corporate tax rate.
7. Fixed asset return.

The first three drivers are those most influenced by external customer and market pressures and consequently we shall concentrate on them in order to remain within the scope of this book.

A company that can successfully influence these value drivers favourably will improve its shareholder value. Many companies have built models which relate the impact of a value driver on the share value of the enterprise. For example, one well-known multibillion dollar global drinks manufacturer has calculated that increasing sales by 1 per cent per annum can influence their share price by $4.00, and that for every $250m they take off their overheads, thereby increasing operating margins, their share price will improve by $1.75.

Some people remain sceptical of the validity of such models in a market which often reacts in the most unpredictable of ways. Few would disagree, however, that much of the model is common sense. A continual downward trend in sales is often a sure sign that a company is past its peak and in decline. You've seen it many times before. First, the organisation withdraws from unprofitable business, then they use the income from those disposals to hide poor profitability. Before you know it, the company has lost market share, shrunk to half its former size and is never likely to recover again.

A company may begin to counter falling sales by discounting and by so doing force itself into a commodity trap with significantly reduced margin and poor profitability. The company produces more, and employees have to work harder, but overall profitability may actually go down.

In another scenario, the company may have enjoyed many boom years and, as a result, have taken on bloated overheads and unaffordable costs. Without reducing these costs, margins will remain uncomfortably small.

Consider the pharmaceutical sector. There, companies have enjoyed decades of growth and comfortable operating margins. Then along came managed care with tough new procurement policies by the healthcare providers. It is perhaps no surprise that margins have begun to erode and the underlying trend in the share price has deteriorated, under-performing the market by some considerable way. Figure 5.1 shows Wellcome's share price in the year 1993/94.

And what of value duration? Rover, the big UK success story of the decade had a successful range of cars, increasing sales and healthy margins. Yet despite its success, management estimated that four or five years down the track, Rover would need $2bn in cash to launch a new range, an unacceptably short value duration for a small national car manufacturer. Thus the acquisition by BMW, sought by its parent British Aerospace, made a great deal of sense as British Aerospace might not have been able to sustain the damaging effect Rover could have had on their future shareholder value.

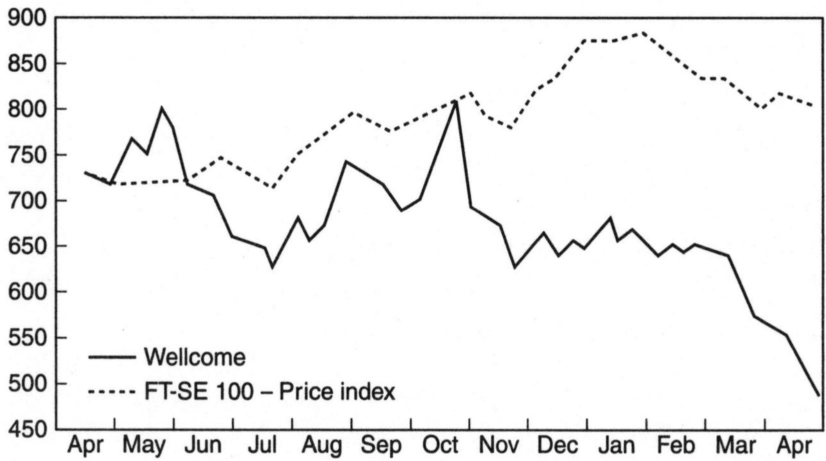

Figure 5.1 Wellcome, an example of a declining share price in the pharmaceutical sector.

CUSTOMER MANAGEMENT AND SHAREHOLDER VALUE

Any percentage increase in sales is governed by organic growth and new products or markets. It is clear that to rely on an increase in sales from organic growth in mature OECD economies is unlikely to be successful while we suffer from low GDP growth and unrelenting recessionary pressures. Customer retention is therefore our main means of securing profitable sales growth for the foreseeable future. If we were to get better at stemming the flow of customers who leave us every year for competitors, then we stand to enjoy a net gain in sales revenue. In other words, if we increase loyalty, repeat purchases go up and so does our revenue curve.

My team at Price Waterhouse aims to reduce lost proposals from one in three to one in 2.5 by improving client retention, representing a net improvement of 17 per cent. A mobile telecommunications provider worked to improve their retention by 5 per cent from 65 per cent to 70 per cent with an eventual goal of achieving 85 per cent retention over seven years, a projected increase in sales therefore of 3 per cent per annum.

Operating margins are also increased by improving customer retention as it costs up to ten times more to acquire new customers than to maintain an existing one. This is borne out by the statistic that a 2 per cent improvement in customer retention is equivalent in profitability terms to a 10 per cent reduction in overheads.

Equally important, the organisation may need to examine its current level of marketing and selling expenditure and establish whether it adds value to the customer. In our pharmaceutical example, managed care organisations want fewer salespeople 'walking the corridors' but more technical seminars. The starting point for any supplier in this sector is value.

Loyalty can also help extend a product or service's value duration which is the period over which it generates positive cash flows. For example, look at Burmah Castrol's lubricant brands. During the early 1990s when most oil companies were hard pressed to make a profit in this highly competitive market, Castrol actually increased its prices and maintained its worldwide market share. It is clear that for

Castrol's customers no substitute will do. The company's long-term investments in the brand have paid off handsomely.

The car industry is notorious for short value durations of only a few years. But clever marketing has kept Rover's mini, the compact car launched in 1959, alive 35 years later in a design almost identical to the original. Now promoted to the wealthy fashion conscious in Tokyo and the chic set in Paris, the car seems to go on and on and may very well be with us into the next century.

In service-intensive industries such as the financial services, adding customer service features can help extend the value duration of certain offerings. In the UK banking sector many of the major clearing banks offered home banking services, all of which were generally regarded as flops within months of their launch. Then along came First Direct's telephone banking service, with well-trained customer service staff able to answer calls 24 hours a day, 365 days a year, and you had an instant success with numbers growing to half a million customers and thousands more joining every week.

BENCHMARKING THE VALUE DRIVERS

We can use benchmarks to indicate areas where we may want to initiate change and thereby influence the value drivers.

First, statistical benchmarks will give us a quick idea of where the company stands in relation to its competitors. From them we may find our sales growth slowing more than that of competitors or others growing market share faster.

Take the case of Hewlett Packard. Of the three computer vendors – Hewlett Packard, IBM, and Digital, Hewlett Packard has outstripped its rivals by having more than 50 per cent of its revenue coming from non-computer sales, non-discretionary expenditure or maintaining office systems such as printers and peripherals. Because of the extensive installed base of its office equipment and its integration into office supplies to keep the equipment operational, Hewlett Packard is in the fortunate position of having a value duration longer than other vendors. Furthermore, it has slashed its overheads way ahead of its competitors to continue to maximise its margins and yet stay price competitive (Figure 5.2).

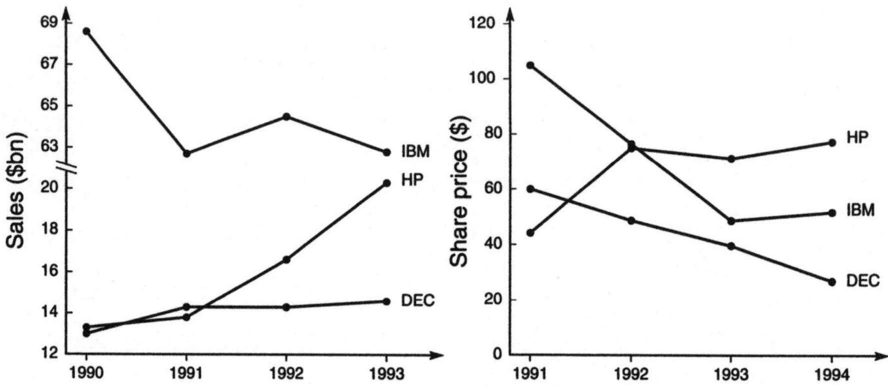

Figure 5.2 Contrasting performances of share price and sales income for IBM, Digital and Hewlett Packard.

Revenue per employer at Hewlett Packard is $300,000 compared with $150,000 at Digital. Little wonder therefore that shareholder value at IBM and Digital has plummeted in relation to Hewlett Packard.

But benchmarking within an industry alone to diagnose problems which affect shareholder value may not provide all the answers. Going back to our earlier pharmaceutical example, most pharmaceutical companies, with their large overheads, face the scourge of managed care's purchasing pressures, making it difficult for them to maintain revenue growth and stay profitable. Statistical benchmarks reveal that their marketing expenditure accounts for 45–50 per cent of their costs – completely unaffordable if they wish to stay in business for the foreseeable future.

They need to look outside, in comparative sectors, to see how other organisations allocate their marketing expenditure. A good example will be found in computer software. It shares the similar problems of high R&D costs, a relatively complex product, low manufacturing expenditure and sales often encountered through intermediaries. In that sector we would be more familiar with marketing expenditure at 15–25 per cent of total costs.

Table 5.1

Customer-related value driver	*Customer-related statistical benchmarks*	*Customer-related process benchmarks*
Percentage increase in sales	Revenue increase/decrease	Review process for determining customer understanding
	New customers	Determining the price/ service risk
	Customer attrition	
	Customer satisfaction	How customer relationships are managed
	Units sold	
	Product lines per customer	
Operating margin	Average selling margins	Integration of marketing and sales
	Margins by segments	Quality of intermediaries
	Sales, marketing expenditure	Effectiveness of selling
	Discounts to intermediaries	
	Customer profitability	
Value duration	Value duration for core products	Customer trends
	Value duration by product	Degree of substitution

An example of how we might use both statistical and process benchmarks to evaluate a customer-related value driver is given in Table 5.1.

Statistical benchmarks such as annual customer attrition, customer satisfaction, units of sales and new customer accounts will position a company against its competition. Low satisfaction scores, combined with falling sales, will indicate, for example, that the company has issues around quality or meeting customer needs. Conversely, rising sales and falling customer satisfaction will be an early warning of trouble to come (Figure 5.3).

Process benchmarks will help the company evaluate the way it goes about understanding customers, determining customer satisfaction

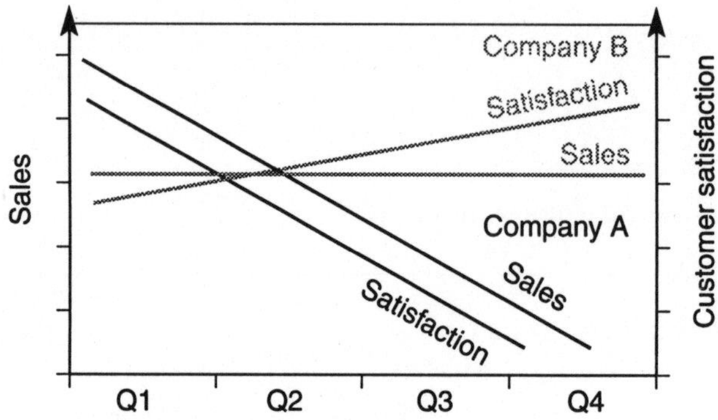

Company A: Falling customer satisfaction and sales revenue. Dissatisfied customers take their business elsewhere.

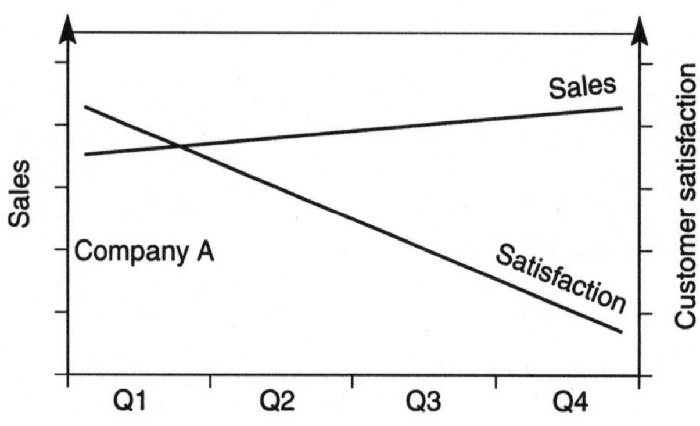

Company A: Falling customer satisfaction and rising sales. Breeding potential problems for the future. How long before sales begin to plummet.

Figure 5.3 Two examples of problems building up. Falling sales and falling satisfaction indicates arrogance or complacency. Address the problem of satisfaction and sales may improve. You could tackle falling sales directly by, say, discounting, but that would harm operating margins. The second example of rising sales but falling satisfaction needs attention right away to address problems with falling sales later.

and managing customer relationships. It may discover, in our pharmaceutical example, that customers' expectations of the service versus price, will have changed. In the meantime the company continues to assume that customers' needs are as they were perhaps five years ago (Figure 5.4).

It would be useful to discover how best practice companies might solve the pharmaceutical problem. The process of understanding customers shows us how to review customers' requirements and to meet service and price criteria. We need to be able to answer questions such as these:

- What value does the customer place on regular sales calls?
- What value is associated with technical seminars?
- What services will the customer pay for?
- Can we segment the market to take account of the changes in customer behaviour?

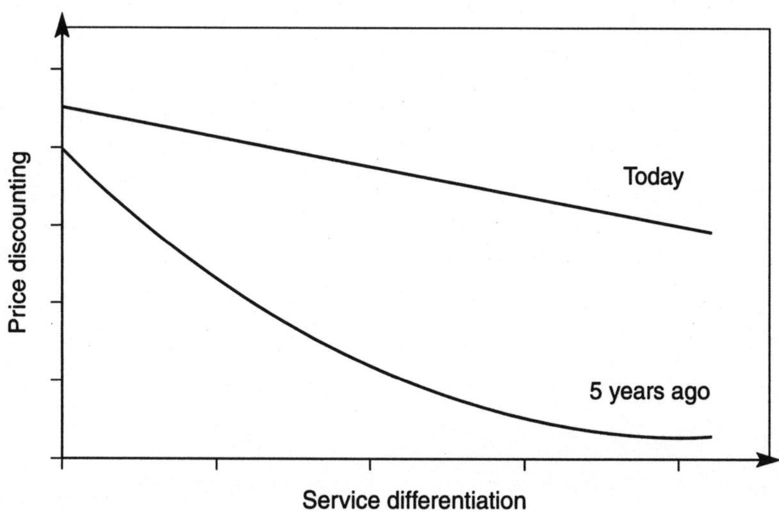

Figure 5.4 One of the key components of understanding customers is to know the changing relationship between price and service. Service does not always add value in the customers' view. Two views illustrated in the graph, now and five years ago.

We could compare how other companies in comparative sectors have responded to similar market characteristics. While companies in our own sector may continue with a product-driven approach to segmenting the market, others facing similar pressures may have adopted different methods of segmentation based on, perhaps, sensitivity to pricing. These other companies may also have begun to introduce speed and responsiveness as a service differentiator, while the role of their sales and marketing teams may have taken on a more technical selling role. Table 5.2 suggests the relationship between market response characteristics and comparisons within the same sector and comparative sectors.

Table 5.2

Market response characteristics	*Sector comparisons*	*Comparative sectors*
Segmentation	Product driven	Price consciousness
Service differentiators	Product education	Speed
Role of Sales and Marketing	More contact time	Technical selling
Role of intermediaries	Closer ties	Closer ties

With regard to operating margins, statistical benchmarks would indicate average selling margins, appropriate margins by segments, discounts to intermediaries and customer profitability, whereas process benchmarks would allow us to examine the effectiveness of our marketing and sales teams. Clearly, if we were to spot any correlation between poor margins and low effectiveness of marketing, then these would indicate areas for immediate action.

SHAREHOLDER VALUE AND THE RELATIONSHIP TO THE KEY DRIVERS

Building a robust model which accurately relates shareholder value to its relationship with the key drivers is considered by some to be an art form rather than economic science. In the absence of such a model it would be enough for management to make a number of simple assumptions about their key drivers:

1. A company with products in an emerging high-growth market such as electronics, communications or media may be expected to produce a double-digit sales growth rate consistent with the expectations of the demand for these hi-tech items.

   At the other extreme, a large well-established company in mature markets may be regarded equally if it succeeds in small increments of sales growth. Going for growth at the expense of all else, such as product or service quality, merely hands competitors the golden opportunity to grow their long-term revenue at your expense.
2. Expectations on operating margins also have a relationship to the type of market in which a company trades. High-growth companies would be expected to have higher operating margins than their more mature counterparts. Consequently, the latter organisations have to work harder at controlling their marketing, selling and customer service expenditure.
3. High-growth companies such as the software games suppliers, would tend to have shorter value durations and they must continually seek to find opportunities to extend the value durations of existing products and services.

   Mature companies such as the utilities would have longer value durations and would have to take fewer short-term actions to extend their periods when they generate cash.

Depending on where your business falls between these two extremes, the reaction to analysing your value drivers, taken together with the benchmarks referred to above, will determine the action you need to take to change.

At any given point in time your enterprise will need to react more vigorously to close the gap for a particular value driver. Many oil companies today greatly need to downsize their fixed overheads and operating expenses in order to improve margins. British Petroleum began this exercise four years ago and in the last two years their shareholder value has more than doubled.

Global telecommunications companies like AT&T need to continue to extend their sales growth in existing and new markets around the world. Software giants like Microsoft and Oracle need to work at extending the value durations of their existing database and applications software as well as launching new products such as multimedia.

Finally, some companies may need to tackle all three of the value drivers which are influenced by market forces. The pharmaceutical companies will have a huge challenge on their hands not only to grow sales and reduce costs, but also to extend their value durations through new and existing products.

Reacting to these value drivers will involve managing change in the business faster and in a more integrated way than ever before. We discuss now an approach to customer-driven change management which will help organisations react to the needs of the three market-influenced value drivers.

THE MANAGEMENT OF CHANGE

In the 1970s, organisations began to introduce project management techniques to realise large capital-intensive infrastructure projects and the concept was soon adopted for a variety of 'soft' projects, from marketing campaigns to social welfare programmes. Project management techniques were recognised for their ability to identify and code the complex inter-relationships between activities, and the time-based dependencies on people and agencies, to deliver the tasks for which they were responsible.

Although project management techniques advanced management thinking on the successful completion of projects, by the late 1980s it became apparent that the management of many projects was carried out in parallel with substantial change occurring within the organisation and in the external environment of competition, regulation and global economics. Often, human factors were found to be behind project failures and there began a recognition that people had to feel motivated and involved in any major project affecting them. Project management techniques alone were incapable of this added complexity and the management of change began to be recognised as a specialised subject in itself.

The management of change requires recognition of the following characteristics:

- Change is a continuous process and project managers must always be in touch with these changes.

- The people who have to live with the changes, be they customers, frontline teams or any other 'stakeholder' in the enterprise, must be involved. Therefore the most successful projects are not by imposition of the changes but by consensus on the best way forward.
- The process of identifying the new vision, outcome or objectives of serving customers must involve a process of improving, simplifying or re-engineering the way we currently maintain relationships with customers.
- There are four irreducible steps to managing any change project:
  - An understanding of the current processes or relationships with customers.
  - A view of the future and what processes must change.
  - The implementation of the changes in the most holistic manner possible.
  - An assessment of the successful implementation of the changed process.

The four steps in conveying what is best referred to as 'customer-driven change' are illustrated in Figure 5.5.

TWO EXAMPLES OF THE DIFFICULTY OF CHANGE

The *Wall Street Journal* ran two stories of companies who had apparently mismanaged change. Consider their example of Avon cosmetics, the $4bn company that's been doing business in roughly the same way for over a hundred years. It believes that customer retention is the key to its success but in the words of its Chief Executive Officer, James Preston, '... change we must, and change we will ...'.

The company has sold cosmetics via a door-to-door sales force, mostly consisting of housewives, who are paid by commission. But times have changed. Fewer women stay at home to receive door-to-door callers and many have begun to buy their cosmetics at supermarkets. As a result, Avon has experienced weakening sales, narrowing margins and a product offer that would appear to be reaching the end of its maturity.

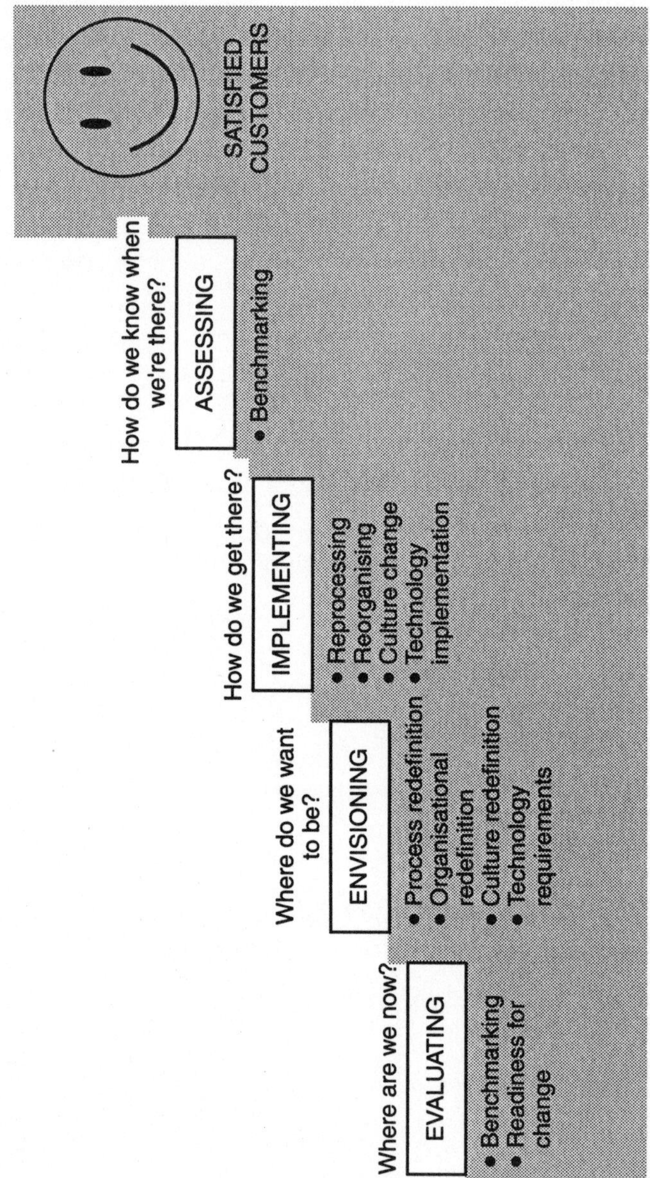

Figure 5.5 The four irreducible steps in managing change. In the first step we evaluate our current postion and benchmarking plays an important part. In the next step we develop a vision of the future, driven by customer needs – the processes we need to deliver our service mission. During implementation we need to put in place the new culture, organisation, skills and technology to support the vision. Finally, we need a mechanism for assessing how we're doing in our process of change – again an important role for benchmarking.

In response to this threat, Avon spent $35m on a national advertising campaign, reported by the *Wall Street Journal* to be the largest in history, to publicise a direct mail sales campaign in a bid to begin the process of creating new sales channels, improving margins and downplaying the role of the door-to-door sales force. Sales representatives' commissions and incentives were cut.

In 1993, pre-tax profits from Avon's US business fell 22 per cent despite reducing headcount and undertaking other cost-cutting initiatives. Marketing analysts believe that Avon's failure in managing change was in failing to understand their customer motivation for buying Avon products and the motivation of their frontline teams. Avon had failed to manage change in the integrated manner necessary to mitigate the internal and external risk of failure.

Historically, Avon 'ladies' had formed strong friendships with many of their customers who, in turn, proved to be loyal customers. But when a representative moved or left her job, her customers usually took their business elsewhere, to the supermarket. The sad point is that Avon's brand image was not strong enough to exist on its own with a disincentivised sales force and falling morale.

Avon isn't the only company to experience getting new customer initiatives wrong. $18bn United Parcels of America recently introduced new improvements to its customer service by offering earlier guaranteed package arrival times and higher limits on package weights. Although popular with customers, the employees reacted angrily with lawsuits and walkouts. The problem was that they felt unhappy with the introduction of new technology, the disruption to their delivery schedules and the heavier weights they had to carry.

The Avon and United Parcels' experiences repeat a frequently repeated lesson: when managing change you need to evaluate carefully both customer and employee motivations. In all too many instances management will act in reaction to one or more of the value drivers without paying due regard to all the fields of play for changes being considered.

CUSTOMER-DRIVEN CHANGE MANAGEMENT

At the risk of being wise after the event, let's pursue the Avon example as a case study in how you might manage customer-driven change in your own organisation.

EVALUATE – WHERE ARE YOU NOW?

The first step of the change management process is to evaluate the problem and how the organisation currently conducts its business. The three market-related shareholder value drivers of 'sales', 'margins' and 'duration' should have given Avon's management serious concern.

Benchmarking would have been the initiator for understanding the existing situation. Comparisons with Mary Kay, Avon's closest competitor, would show that at that time the company was also market testing their own direct-mail catalogue. However, they were adopting an approach whose objective was not to disturb the relationships with the direct sales force. The commissions from new customer sales were to be directed through to local sales representatives and catalogue items were slightly different from those offered by the door-to-door sales force, so as to avoid head-to-head competition.

Further benchmarking of Avon's customers would have revealed that stripping away the door-to-door sales channels and the relationship-based selling which it had created would leave the products without an independent brand identity. The company would have to create a separate brand identity for the direct-mail products if it was to succeed in the marketplace.

Had Avon benchmarked the five customer processes (described in detail in chapter 3: 'Understanding customers' needs', 'Managing customer relationships', 'Delivering service through people', 'Managing dissatisfaction', and 'Measuring satisfaction)' they would have realised the need to make some substantial progress in being a customer-led organisation. The fact was that, despite changes in the customer behaviour – more women going out to work and increased competition from supermarkets – the key selling channels and mechanisms for delivery had remained unchanged.

Another part of the evaluation stage would be to appreciate the readiness for change in the organisation and the position of the key 'stakeholders' in bringing about change (Figure 5.6).

The head of Avon's US business was violently opposed to the direct-mail initiative and set up his own competing programme. The project team at company headquarters failed to take this powerful influence along with them. The sales force, faced with dwindling commissions, was also an opposing force with most to lose and whose views had not

Stakeholders	Readiness to change			Action points
	Welcome change	Neutral attitude	Strongly opposed	
Customers	Maintain ●			Continue to promote service improvements
Regional management			● Positive action to gain acceptance	Stress impact on future loss of revenue
Sales force			● Positive action to gain commitment	Stress opportunity to earn improved remuneration
Intermediaries		Strengthen ●		Promote enhanced future relationship, less intermediaries by then
Support staff		Strengthen ●		No immediate action
Senior management	Strengthen ●			Identify potential improvement in shareholder value

Figure 5.6 An analysis of stakeholders and their readiness to change. Key stakeholders are assessed in terms of their attitude to the changes being proposed and the action that needs to be taken to overcome resistance.

been accommodated. Customers, their close allies, although probably welcoming some aspects of the new offering would not have supported the prospect of losing the regularity of contact with their friendly Avon 'ladies', established over several years.

So we can see that assessing the readiness for change of each stakeholder will provide the likely barriers and obstacles which need to be overcome during implementation.

THE VISION FOR CHANGE

Most change projects today rely on changing the processes by which the organisation serves its customers. Processes have become recognised as a more effective and sustainable way of engineering change because they tackle the core of the organisation's objectives to serve customers and to be profitable in so doing. Changing functions limits the issue to remain within existing organisational boundaries and is thus far too limiting to bring about fundamental improvements in the way we deal with customers.

Picture this scenario. *Sales* see their objective in life as selling to the customer. *Finance* believe they are the guardians of ensuring that the operation's finances don't run out of control. *Marketing* see their role as understanding customers and formulating new promotions. *Management* regard their role as providing leadership, frequently from a plush office in a smart part of town. *Customer Service*, when boxed in somehow among these groupings frequently suffers.

We have all experienced what happens. Salespeople sell products to customers who probably can't afford to pay or keep up the premiums. Finance chase with ridiculous vigour inappropriate debt with long-standing loyal customers, and management never get to meet customers and hear their gripes at first hand.

Figure 5.7 shows how reviewing a business as a set of processes transcends traditional functional business operations.

A process is usually a collection of activities carried out with a defined set of outputs for which there is always a customer, be it an internal or external one. Similarly, there will always be 'suppliers' of information, goods or services to the process. Figure 5.8 summarises this concept.

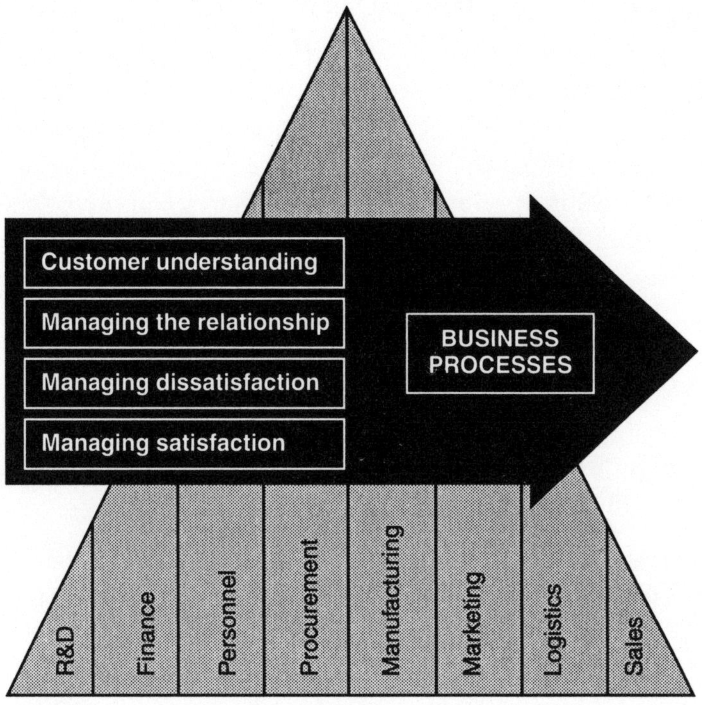

Figure 5.7 Processes transcend functional boundaries.

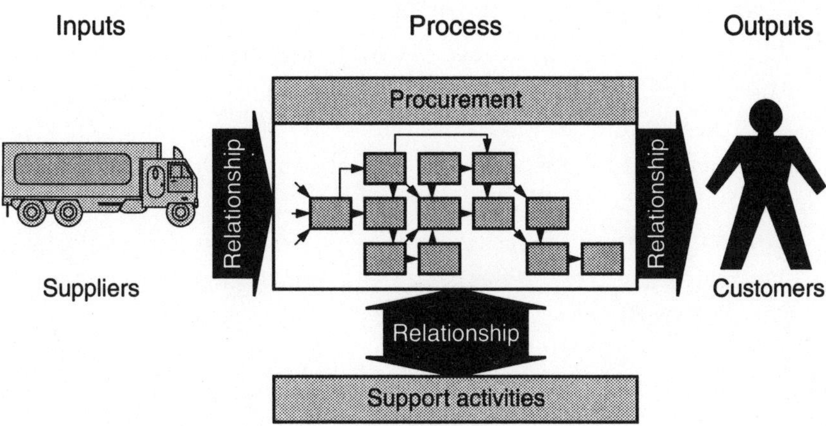

Figure 5.8 How a process works.

An organisation should be able to define its customer processes by assembling together representatives of all the relevant functions in order to map the way they work together in pursuit of a common process. Mapping these processes allows cross-functional teams collectively to challenge the complexity of existing working practices and suggest ways of improving customer service and resulting customer relationships.

Sadly, *business process engineering*, as the technique has now been labelled, was seized upon by systems designers and most attempts at innovation or radical redesign in establishing new processes was swamped in a morass of process and activity diagrams.

Kept at its most simple, process redesign is still one of the most powerful techniques to develop a vision for enhanced customer service. It has the following steps:

1. Define the key customer processes relevant to your organisation, for example 'managing the relationship' or 'managing dissatisfaction'.
2. Through benchmarking, ask customers how they rate your processes and confirm those findings with your own frontline teams.
3. Select one or two processes which you most urgently need to change, and set up design groups which are cross-functional. Each group should be co-ordinated by a 'process owner' who must be someone with a passion for changing that process.
4. Produce a map of 'the way we do it now' and 'the way we ought to do it in future', being as radical as possible and with the customer always in mind. Temper radicalism later only if it is a major barrier to change or gaining acceptability with other stakeholders. Only delve into detail if it is necessary in order to understand the process and the implications for change.
5. Communicate your redesigned processes to all stakeholders including customers. Re-evaluate your proposals if you encounter major obstacles.

Let's review the Avon case study again, and see how they might have gone about envisioning a change to the organisation.

The project team formed to engineer change should have included the major power brokers or stakeholders. This top team would have been involved in a high-level definition of the key processes which interface with the customer and the issues and opportunities facing Avon for each process.

This would have been an early step in establishing ownership and commitment to any emerging changes at later stages. These early meetings or workshops would have reviewed the benchmarking findings and assigned them for consideration by the re-engineering teams.

Individuals to lead the re-engineering of each key process would be nominated and agreed by the senior team. Each process re-engineering team would include representatives of each stakeholder group and they would begin to map each process in the way the organisation currently conducts its business.

At this stage the Avon change team would have begun to form an appreciation of how the energies and resources of the employees are channelled into fulfilling orders and meeting customers' needs. It would have become apparent that the life of an Avon 'lady' is a labour-intensive and demanding one. Many work 12–14 hours a day, doing a variety of administrative and order despatch tasks other than calling on customers. Redesign and automation of these tasks, allowing representatives to spend more time calling on customers, would undoubtedly give rise to more sales.

Benchmarking would have also given the change team an idea of the existing 'tribal culture'. Where is Avon on the continuum between customer arrogance and customer passionate? Different levels of the organisation may correspond to a different culture and the challenge of the change teams will be to develop a homogenous culture.

In developing a vision for the future, the re-engineering teams would have adopted a vision of the way they believe the business processes could be best improved. This would include eliminating tasks, taking on more responsibility, broadening responsibilities, automating manually intensive tasks and generally taking on best practice ideas generated by the benchmarking studies.

Here it would be important to involve best practice from within the organisation. The US business, for example, gets over half of its revenue from just over 15 per cent of the sales force, with some high performing representatives single handedly accounting for up to $0.5m in sales. These people in themselves embody the competencies and ideas which Avon needs to propagate across its network. They would also have the credibility and respect of the employees.

Also, involving the customer in the redesign process is important to ensure that emerging proposals do not meet resistance from these key stakeholders. Customer focus groups, held to produce opportunities for improving the Avon offering, might reveal that the time lag between placing the order and receiving the goods is inappropriate at a time when you can obtain competing products 'off the shelf' or within 24 hours.

The redesigned processes carry with them implications for organisation restructuring, job redefinition, changes in the management culture of the organisation and the requirements for new systems and information technology. In missing out any of these essential components the organisation weakens its ability to implement an integrated solution to the changes required. Benchmarking is important to establish the precedence of previous examples of each working in practice.

By this stage the target culture should have been defined. If Avon wants to correspond to a customer passionate culture then what are the tribal values it must change to adopt the new culture?

IMPLEMENTATION – HOW DO WE GET THERE?

Implementation is the point at which many change projects falter or fail. While ideas may be a dime a dozen, it is only their implementation that provides the Midas touch. The greater the rigour of the previous stages of evaluation and envisioning the change, the greater the chances will be of a successful implementation. The more Avon involved its key stakeholders in the early stages of its programme, the more they would have understood their existing business processes. The better their benchmarks of best practice and the better their understanding of customers, the greater would have been their chances of success.

During implementation the organisation defines the re-engineered processes in greater detail in order to define new job responsibilities and changes to the organisation, new control and authority levels and the new systems and information technology required to support the targeted changes. Implementing change can be highly disruptive if it creates uncertainty and therefore it is essential to communicate clearly to all employees the planned implementation and how each one is going to be affected.

Customers should be informed of all changes likely to affect them. Communication is done best, and appreciated most, when it is carried out verbally by frontline teams. Early reaction from customers to the changes should be recorded and the implementation teams made aware of any negative consequences.

Changing to the new target culture may need to begin with small but significant steps to dismantle the old style and bring in the new. That might mean that the Chief Executive Officer himself goes on a few sales calls every year to keep in touch with customers and to signal change to the representatives. Top-performing Avon 'ladies' may need to be given greater public recognition of their achievements in addition to financial incentives and customer satisfaction may need to be included in future remuneration packages.

The final step of training and people development needs to be integrated with the other implementation initiatives. If only the top 15 per cent of representatives correspond to the best practice framework of the future, then the competencies of the remaining 85 per cent will need to be evaluated, training being provided to those most willing to learn. It may be considered that future recruits should be subject to tougher screening criteria and the status of being an Avon 'lady' be elevated.

ASSESSING – HOW DO WE KNOW WE'RE GETTING THERE?

Once again benchmarking plays a key role in telling us if the change programme is working. The process benchmarks would indicate improvements to the internal customer-related activities, while customer satisfaction benchmarks would monitor the external perceptions. Customer perceptions of shorter delivery lead times and more regular customer calls will be monitored by independent research and verified by frontline teams.

More statistically oriented benchmarks of the performance of key processes such as billing, sales per representative, profitability per sales area and complaints per 1,000 customers will also be important to assess operational performance. In addition, the assessment of the three market-related value drivers will be the ultimate test of the viability of the programme of change. For example, has our year-on-year sales growth improved? Have margins increased? Have we revitalised interest in mature products?

On reading this chapter you should ask the following questions of your enterprise:

1. Are we clear as to which of the customer value drivers we need to concentrate on to enhance shareholder value?
2. Is there any other organisation we know that has made a particularly good job of working on similar value drivers to enhance share value and can we learn from them?
3. In implementing changes necessary to improve share value have we understood the implications for all stakeholders?
4. Has our evaluation taken account of all the following benchmarks: (a) the service strategy; (b) the culture; (c) the processes and individual transactions which make up the service proposition?
5. Do we intend involving all stakeholders in developing a vision of what needs to change?
6. Are our processes developed from the point of view of the customer?
7. Does each process have an improvement measure which would be discernable by the customer?
8. Do we intend using benchmarks to measure the improvement in our change programme?
9. Do we have an idea of the anticipated improvements the changes will bring on shareholder value?
10. Does the change plan have clear leadership?

Answers

- *Yes* to more than 7 questions and you should we well placed to manage change with the aim of enhancing share value.
- *Yes* to between 4 and 6 questions and you have some more work to do. The hardest areas are the involvement of stakeholders and the bit we don't always do terribly well.
- *Yes* to less than 4 questions and you have considerably more work to do.

6

CASE STUDIES IN BENCHMARKING

In this chapter we cover two case studies in benchmarking: a multisector study concentrating on process benchmarking; and a sector specific study in the pharmaceuticals 'over the counter' sector. You may find some of the experiences useful in deciding your customer service benchmarking strategy.

THE MULTISECTOR CUSTOMER EXCELLENCE BENCHMARKING PROJECT

In 1993 we held a forum in London of 200 companies to discuss the customer management issues facing organisations. The event was organised around a series of workshops and seminars. The organisations involved in addressing customer management initiatives selected participation at four workshops out of a list of twelve topics which were as follows:

1. How do you engender a customer-focused organisation? (chosen by 68 per cent)
2. How do you benchmark customer management and act upon it? (chosen by 65 per cent)
3. How do we re-engineer the customer back into our business? (chosen by 50 per cent)
4. How do we differentiate in commoditised markets? (chosen by 46 per cent)
5. How do we go about understanding customers? (chosen by 42 per cent)
6. What is best practice in handling customer complaints? (chosen by 40 per cent)

7. How do we make our sales force more effective? (chosen by 35 per cent)
8. How can we ensure we are getting value for money from marketing expenditure? (chosen by 28 per cent)
9. Do total quality programmes really work? (chosen by 26 per cent)
10. How do you make IT deliver world-class customer management? (chosen by 25 per cent)
11. What is best practice in the use of marketing information systems? (chosen by 25 per cent)
12. How do you go about entering new global markets? (chosen by 8 per cent)

One of the conclusions from the forum was a request by the attendees, subsequently called the '200 Club', for us to initiate a benchmarking project. Although more than 80 per cent of the '200 Club' had begun to perform benchmarking in their own organisations, less than 10 per cent felt they were making any real advances in their customer management as a result.

These were some of the difficulties people faced in successfully conducting customer benchmarking:

- Setting up benchmarking studies was time-consuming, particularly for senior management occupied with the day-to-day pressures of running the business. The greatest amount of abortive time seemed to have been spent in finding out which organisations to benchmark against and, perhaps more importantly, which people in those organisations would co-operate most freely in exchange of information.
- There was a resistance towards sharing best practice in some organisations which considered they had nothing to learn from the outside world: 'Why should we benchmark, we already know we're the best'.
- Smaller to medium-sized enterprises had particular difficulty with accessing bigger corporations because of the inherent arrogance in the latter to acknowledge they had anything in common.
- Many had difficulty in establishing a method to ensure comparability of results – how could an airline compare itself with, say, the postal service or the stock exchange?

- How did one get beyond the superficiality of informal discussions into the nitty gritty sharing of ideas on business operations? While it seemed easy to talk broadly about benchmarking over, say, a lunch, there did not seem to be the opportunity to delve into any amount of detail.

DEFINING THE REQUIREMENTS

In order to respond to this request to act as a benchmarking facilitator, we set out to define a set of requirements for benchmarking customer management. We selected a sample of twenty companies to interview in order to come up with these requirements. Our interviews were conducted over a period of four to five months and we arrived at the following specification:

- Process benchmarks should be the focus of this benchmarking initiative. Many companies had already begun to participate in trade or industry-led benchmarking projects and these were almost always statistically oriented. It told you that you were lousy at, say, handling complaints, but it didn't tell you what to do about it.
- It should be cross-industry. There were few new ideas for engineering a step change in service levels within one's own industry. Real breakthroughs would only come from other sectors.
- If the benchmarking facility had to be across industries, then a framework for assessment should be established, which was generic to any industry, and should be used as the common nomenclature for the benchmarking.
- As most benchmarking studies contained inappropriate attention to assessing one's own organisation first, it would be desirable to offer this diagnostic as the initiator to the study of other organisations. This diagnostic should be carried out with reference to worldwide best practice in customer management.
- The study should be multinational with the initial focus on Europe and with an eye on extending the review globally.

Armed with the above specifications we set about constructing a benchmarking proposal for the '200 Club' to consider. We appeared to have the requirement for diagnostics combined with reference to best practice and the need to look across sector. The latter made it easier to seek potential participants as the potential pool of organisations was much larger. The need to adopt a best practice framework, however, was the subject of considerable thought and debate in our team. We appeared to have two options:

1. To adopt an existing framework which had already gained some credibility in self-assessment or quality management.
2. To develop our own framework based on research and experience of consulting engagements over the last five years.

We adopted the former option. We were joined towards the end of 1993 by Mike Crosswell, who had been director of quality with the Carrier group, affiliated to the US parent United Technologies. Mike had implemented the Malcolm Baldridge framework for quality assessment in his previous organisation and he did a good job of convincing us of the suitability of Baldridge for our benchmarking exercise.

Baldridge seemed particularly appropriate because of its strong customer process origins and it being a widely accepted model. Bearing in mind that many of the companies in our '200 Club' had US parents, the need to adopt a framework that had broad acceptability was further emphasised.

At about the same time we also became aware of a number of European-based organisations carrying out self-assessment according to the European Foundation of Quality Management (EFQM). The EFQM model seemed to be a further refinement of Baldridge, with the addition of business results being added to quell criticism that the pursuit of excellence had to be reflected in improved business performance.

We cherry-picked the best out of both models, in a way our own version of benchmarking, and created the five-process model for customer excellence referred to earlier in chapter 3. These were:

- The process of understanding customers.
- The process of managing dissatisfaction.
- The process of measuring satisfaction.
- The process of empowering people who serve customers.
- The process of managing customer relationships.

The above processes had captured about 55 per cent and 50 per cent respectively of the European Quality Award and Baldridge models. They seemed to cover all the generic processes of customer management that we could identify and we carried out a number of iterations internally in the Price Waterhouse network to test the comprehensiveness of the process descriptions.

TESTING THE BENCHMARKING PROPOSALS

Having now found a framework for evaluation we decided to test the proposals once more with our sample of twenty. We had by now, through our exposure to Baldridge and the EQA, become converts to the idea of continual process improvement. The presentations to the companies which had originally defined the specification for the benchmarking project were well received.

We proposed that the benchmarking study be done in modules or units which were capable of being carried out over a week of assessment. This would entail up to two assessors from Price Waterhouse carrying out interviews with the five 'process owners' and following up each interview with an observation of the process actually being executed. So, if a process owner claimed that the organisation had defined service guarantees, then we would ask to see them and how they were being communicated.

We also proposed that, following the assessment, we would produce a report showing scores for each process in the 'approach', 'deployment' and 'results' categories, and follow up later with comparisons with sector and overall winners.

Our sample companies made some useful comments which went into further refinement of the benchmarking prospectus. The comments were as follows:

- People felt comfortable with the generic nature of the processes and applauded the adoption of a world-class model such as Baldridge/EQA. This met most of their requirements for global comparability and diagnostic capability. The idea of an independent assessment was also welcomed by senior managers because there had been some history of previous self-assessments not being rigorous enough. Some organisations declared their intention to link bonuses in future to the benchmarking assessments.

- They felt that it would be important to produce actionable information from the assessment and the provision of a score without backup suggestions on strengths, weaknesses and areas for action would not do full justice to the study.
- They thought the idea of a get together with other participating companies at some point in the programme would further enhance the value of the review.

MARKETING THE STUDY

Having incorporated the second round of comments made, we commenced an initial round of marketing the benchmarking study. Early in this process we sought to get external recognition of the study from well-respected senior managers. Both Mike Grabiner, a senior director at British Telecom, and Peter Sharrock of Reuters, gave their early backing to the study and we issued a press release to launch the initiative. Also, within the Price Waterhouse network we began to publicise the programme using partners with specific client responsibility to raise the benchmarking project with their clients.

We printed a prospectus based on the feedback from our second round of comments and sent this document to all members of our '200 Club'.

TRAINING THE ASSESSORS

We found it necessary to train some thirty assessors across our European network to carry out the evaluations to a common standard. Training sessions were organised for the assessors and the case study of Packaging International, given in chapter 3, was used as the basis of the training.

We were careful only to choose assessors who had themselves a previous background in customer management. Much of the diagnostics required a degree of judgement and we felt that previous experience of the processes under consideration was necessary to arrive at an evaluation.

Process benchmarking is not a precise management science and this was the point at which we encountered certain cultural differences in the degree of comfort with our framework and proposed approach. The greatest difficulty was encountered by our German consultants whose natural inclination would have been to work with a lower level model with greater definition. However, as explained earlier, the need to remain at a generic process level predicated the ability to do this.

THE PILOTS

We had one last step to perform before the evaluation process was ready for a major roll out. We had to perform a couple of pilot assessments so that the benchmarking method could be tested on a real 'live' organisation.

The pilots were a great success with letters of commendation being received from the sponsors. We had very little improvement to make to the process.

THE BENCHMARKING CENTRE

Setting up the core infrastructure to support this programme has been an important part of its success. The benchmarking centre is responsible for logging all results in a database we refer to as 'Knowledgeview'. This is a best practice database which is used to record all benchmarks for key processes in an organisation. Strict security has been imposed to ensure that the results from each organisation participating are kept confidential.

The benchmarking centre also acts as the central help desk for all enquiries and tracks the progress of all interested participants from the initial request for information to production of the final report.

CONDUCTING THE REVIEWS

We usually encourage a senior manager to take ownership of the benchmarking project within a company. We discuss the scope of the exercise in terms of the number of business units covered and the geographical coverage. If the business unit covers a numbers of countries as a single homogeneous market, then the benchmarking study usually mirrors the way the organisation faces the market. If the business unit regards each country as a different market with substantially variable customer-buying characteristics, then each market team would be reviewed independently.

For example, a commodity chemicals producer supplying the styrene market in Europe would be regarded as a single unit for benchmarking purposes. A pharmaceutical company, on the other hand, is governed by different country-dominated buying characteristics and therefore each country operating unit would be reviewed separately.

Process owners are given prior notification of areas to be covered in the interview with them, which usually lasts about three hours. At the interview one assessor conducts the review while another observes the process and provides comment on the interview at its conclusion. This has been invaluable in improving the assessment process, extending the pool of assessors and ensuring uniformity of assessments.

Following the review, the assessors discuss their general conclusions with the senior sponsor and follow up with a written report. The sponsor usually discusses the findings with the senior management team which decides on whether or not to incorporate the action points in their customer management improvement programmes. Many have indicated that they will conduct regular diagnostics to monitor improvement.

CONCLUSIONS

At the time of writing the membership of the benchmarking study has risen to 50 with five or six new companies joining every month. The project has taken the best part of a year to mature. As we roll the study out worldwide we will able to study the cultural differences between customer management practices around the world. Already some of these differences are beginning to emerge and they would provide the basis of interesting research once we have a critical mass of data.

The one overriding learning point in the process so far is that the setting up of the benchmarking initiative has taken nearly 85 per cent of the effort. Conducting the reviews is less than 5 per cent of the effort and doing the analysis and reporting occupy the remaining 10 per cent.

BENCHMARKING IN THE PHARMACEUTICAL SECTOR

In 1992, a group of leading 'over-the-counter' (OTC) drug companies, with operations in the United States, approached Price Waterhouse requesting that we serve as a confidential intermediary to help them compare their performance with each other. They had become familiar with the concepts of organisations transforming themselves to be more responsive to customer needs and sought to do the same in their own organisations. A number had already undertaken benchmarking studies of their own. Their declared intention was to extend benchmarking beyond sporadic and sometimes superficial exercises to a thorough, rigorous and objective process.

We accepted the brief and by the end of 1992 nineteen companies received the first Benchmark '92 Survey. The report compared their performance on 120 key operating measures and over 200 business practices. Following the success of the '92 survey, the '93 survey was commissioned and reported in the spring of that year.

The studies had the simple objective: '... to exchange key performance data and see exactly where we stand relative to our peers. By doing this we will know what level of performance must be attained to become best in class. Those who can use that knowledge effectively will be better able to compete.'

The study had three areas of focus:

1. Key operating ratios.
2. Company and industry trends.
3. Emerging business practices.

The intention was to identify those business practices which lead to superior performance.

BENCHMARK DESIGN

The companies identified three key criteria which were important to them:

1. There should be complete confidentiality of data and at no time should it be apparent that a set of statistics corresponded to a particular company.
2. The data should be comparable between participating organisations.
3. In addition to data, the survey had to produce actionable information to improve business performance.

These were the companies which participated:

American Home Products
Bausch & Lomb
Bristol-Myers Squibb
Burroughs Wellcome
Chattem
CIBA
Combe
Johnson & Johnson/Merck
Care
Lederle
McNwil
Mentholatum
Miles
Pfizer
Procter & Gamble
Rhone-Poulenc Rorer
Sandoz
Schering-Plough
SmithKline Beecham
Sterling Winthrop
Upjohn
Warner Lambert

An early objective was to create a secure process for collecting and securing the most sensitive operating data from each participant. To do this we used our Survey Research Centre in Washington D.C. to co-ordinate the data collection and apply their standards for security which included the following:

- Assigning a confidential code to each participant which then appeared on the company response instead of the company name, thus keeping the analysis 'blind'.

- Transmitting the data without identifying the submitting company's name.
- Using a standalone computer to do the analysis.
- Keeping all data on diskette to prevent any data 'shadowing'.
- Storing all data in locked cabinets within a secured office suite.

To ensure that the survey results would provide value we designed a 'strawman' survey and then reviewed it with thirteen participants to see if it met the criteria originally set by the participants.

CONDUCT OF THE SURVEY

All surveys were questionnaire-driven with careful attention to define the questions asked and to remove ambiguity. A help desk was also set up to answer queries, should they arise. Companies were given a four-week window to complete the questionnaires and a team of experts worked on the analysis over a three-week period following the submission of the data. To achieve comparability of the data we used a series of logic tests. Errors and outliners were brought to the attention of each respondent and the data was corrected. The data was examined in relation to a range of financial results. Using statistical analysis, software over 2000 relationships were tested. For example, the relationship of salesperson's commission to sales growth and the trend of defective returned goods as a percentage of overall revenue were reported.

On reading this chapter you should ask the following questions of your enterprise:

1. Which benchmarking approach do we think we would benefit from most, the sector or the multisector option?
2. Do we have the management resource to conduct the review entirely on our own or should we join an existing club?
3. Do we want to concentrate our efforts at the process level or the statistical level, or both?

4. Who would be the ideal project sponsor for a benchmarking initiative?
5. Is our culture such that we would accept the finding that we have much to do to improve?

Answers

1. Your choice of sector versus multisector will depend on whether you believe you have more to gain from learning how organisations outside your sector carry out best practice in managing customers. Your choice of a sector bias will be determined by your perception that you are already some distance away from best practice among your competitors.
2. Your decision on whether you have the management resource will depend on the strength of relationships you have already established in the target organisations. The fewer the contacts the more time-consuming the set-up. Setting up the benchmarking is 70 per cent of the effort. Join an existing club if it appears well run.
3. Your choice of statistical or process level will depend on the propensity of your management team to react to process information rather than numbers. Some people believe in numbers more than any other piece of information. Statistical benchmarking may also be favoured in cases where no industry data exists on service levels and where this is an area of close competition.
4. The ideal project sponsor would be someone who has a senior executive level of responsibility in the organisation and who is appreciated as an agent of change.
5. Answer this question honestly. Much of the benchmarking effort will be wasted if the organisation is unlikely to react to the findings. You may want to explore areas where there is a greater openness to change and concentrate your efforts there.

APPENDIX I:

A BENCHMARKING PROJECT PLAN

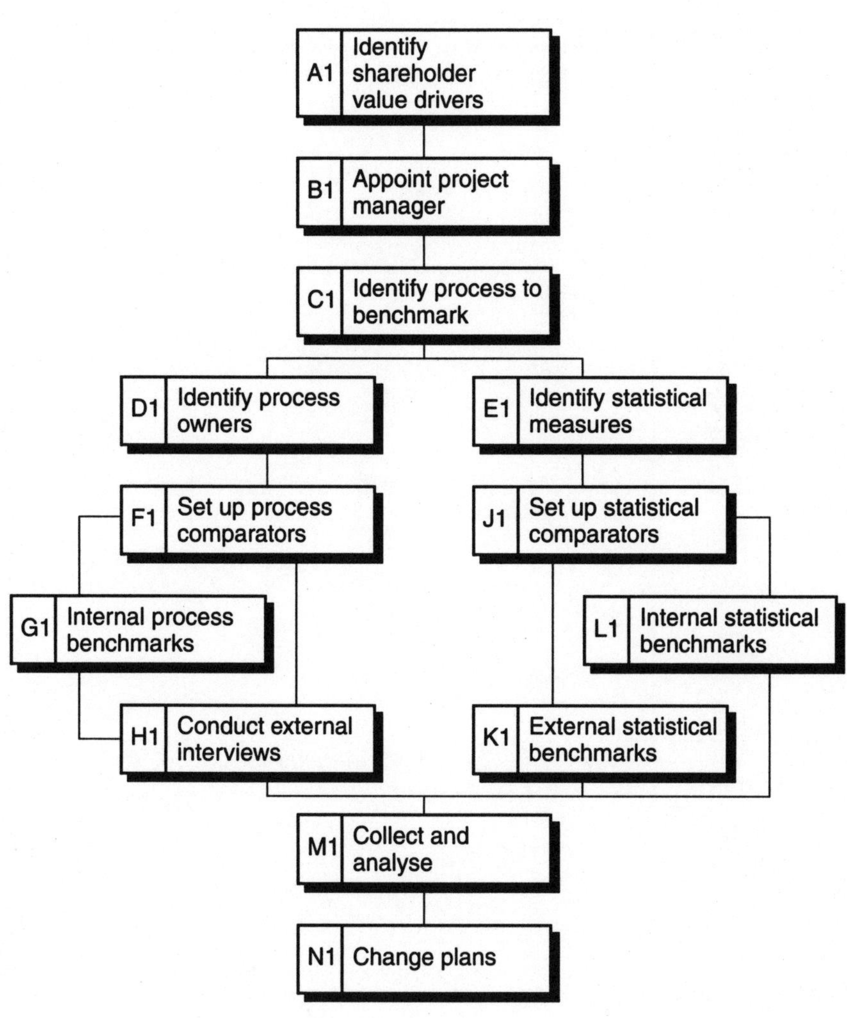

CUSTOMER BENCHMARKING - Activity Sheet

ACTIVITY A1	Identify shareholder value drivers
Objective	*Objective: To perform a high level analysis of the areas which adversely affect shareholder value to help focus benchmarking efforts.*
Inputs	*Company data. Balance sheet. Forecast 3 years. Comparative equivalents for up to 5 other companies. Some should be non-competitors sharing similar characteristics.*
Outputs	*Gap analysis showing areas of significant adverse variance for each value driver.*
Involvement	*Executive, analyst.*
Process	*Preparing and running a model for the key drivers which affect shareholder value. Collecting data and value driven comparisons.*

CUSTOMER BENCHMARKING - Activity Sheet (cont'd)

ACTIVITY B1	Appoint project manager
Objective	*Objective: Appoint a lead manager to co-ordinate the activities of the benchmarking effort.*
Inputs	*CVs of external and internal candidates.*
Outputs	*Specification of role. Communication of appointment.*
Involvement	*Senior managers from customer-related functions.* *Executive sponsor.*
Process	*Executive sponsor consults with managers on most suitable candidate. Reviews both internal and external options.*

CUSTOMER BENCHMARKING - Activity Sheet (cont'd)

ACTIVITY C1	Identify process to benchmark
Objective	*Objective: To focus benchmarking effort on the key processes which are associated with value drivers identified by gap analysis.*
Inputs	*Gap analysis from value-driver comparisons. Other market data on satisfaction, position, pricing, etc.*
Outputs	*Suggested processes for benchmarking. Reasons for choice.*
Involvement	*Key managers with customer contact reponsibility. Executive sponsor. Project manager.*
Process	*Nominated project manager proposes paper showing gap analysis and suggested process for investigation. Hold meeting chaired by sponsor with key managers to agree processes.*

CUSTOMER BENCHMARKING - Activity Sheet (cont'd)

ACTIVITY D1	Identify process owners
Objective	*Objective: To allocate someone responsible for all benchmarking activity and resulting action plans associated with a process.*
Inputs	*Potential candidates who understand relevant process.*
Outputs	*Process owners.*
Involvement	*Executive sponsor.*
Process	*Indentify process owners who appear to be people who want change and see it as a continuous process.* *Leave out those who are happy to maintain the status quo.*

CUSTOMER BENCHMARKING - Activity Sheet (cont'd)

ACTIVITY E1	Identify statistical measures
Objective	*Objective: To indentify the statistical measures associated with each selected process. The statistical measures to be key performance measures.*
Inputs	*Selected processes.*
Outputs	*Measures to be benchmarked.*
Involvement	*Project manager with process owners.*
Process	*For each process selected the process owners identify critical success factors and related key performance measures, usually on key measures.*

CUSTOMER BENCHMARKING - Activity Sheet (cont'd)

ACTIVITY F1	Set up process comparators
Objective	*Objective: To indentify the relevant organisations, internal and external, against which benchmarks are to be conducted and to agree best options for gaining access and conducting study.*
Inputs	• *Competitors most relevant.* • *External organisations sharing similar characteristics.* • *Lists of benchmarking clubs, sector studies and consulting organisations currently undertaking benchmarking.*
Outputs	• *1 or 2 competitor organisations per process.* • *2 or 3 non-competing organisations per process.* • *and benchmarking group or consultant.*
Involvement	*Project manager assisted where necessary by process owners.*
Process	*The project manager reviews the selected processes and identifies no more than 2 competing organisations which may be prepared to participate. Similarly non-competing organisations most admired for their excellence in a process should be selected. Contacts best made by referral. At the same time the availability of a suitable benchmarking group may be sought to facilitate access or consultants would facilitate introductions.*

CUSTOMER BENCHMARKING - Activity Sheet (cont'd)

ACTIVITY G1	Internal process benchmarks
Objective	*Objective: To prepare an understanding of the organisation's own benchmarks and to compare best practice within the organisation's area operating units.*
Inputs	• *Operating units using similar processes.* • *Review method for comparisons.*
Outputs	• *Analysis of best practice in organisation.* • *Strengths and weaknesses of each operating unit in comparison to process.*
Involvement	*Operating unit managers, processes owners.*
Process	*Before beginning external benchmarks it is necessary to understand internal benchmarks. Process owners facilitate benchmarking reveiws in organisational units showing similar processes. A framework or structure for the review must be prepared beforehand. The benchmarking output for each process is prepared by the process owners who compare best practice across the organisation and submit the report to the executive sponsor.*

CUSTOMER BENCHMARKING - Activity Sheet (cont'd)

ACTIVITY H1	Conduct external interviews
Objective	*Objective: To compare the company's best operational processes with those of external organisations and to agree where best practice exists.*
Inputs	• *Best processes being followed by company's operational units.* • *Structure for companies refined from internal benchmarks.* • *Meeting schedules.*
Outputs	• *Agree best practices.* • *Strengths, weaknesses of organisations.*
Involvement	*Process owners and counterparts in benchmarked organisation.*
Process	*The company chooses only those operational units which constitute best practice for comparisons. Process owners meet their counterparts in benchmarked organisation to compare the approach, and the business results produced.*

CUSTOMER BENCHMARKING - Activity Sheet (cont'd)

ACTIVITY J1	Set up statistical comparators
Objective	*Objective: To identify relevant organisations which may participate in a statistical questionnaire-driven benchmarking survey.*
Inputs	• *Directories of relevant companies in sector.* • *Identify trade groups.* • *Exploratory letter to organisations selected.* • *Selected processes and associated statistical measures.* • *Definitions of each measure.*
Outputs	*Selected companies to be included in postal questionnaire.*
Involvement	*Project manager.*
Process	*Selecting and approaching a number of companies within sector to participate. Usually using the services of a consultant or trade group to ensure acceptance and confidentiality of data. Also state benefits to be gained by consolidated results.*

CUSTOMER BENCHMARKING - Activity Sheet (cont'd)

ACTIVITY K1	External statistical benchmarks
Objective	*Objective: To obtain benchmarks of other comparable organisations at a level which measures the performance of each customer management process.*
Inputs	• *Comparable organisations based on sector and similar process.* • *Questionnaires refined from internal statistical benchmarking.*
Outputs	• *Returned questionnaries.*
Involvement	*Process manager, process owners.*
Process	*Questionnaires are prepared detailing the statistical benchmarks required for each process being investigated, e.g. customer understanding process - number of customer segments, frequency of third party surveys. These are agreed by process owners. Mailing by project manager to comparable organisations, always offering something in return.*

CUSTOMER BENCHMARKING - Activity Sheet (cont'd)

ACTIVITY L1	Internal statistical benchmarks
Objective	Objective: To obtain benchmarks of the customer process within the organisation and to obtain the best statistical performance in the group.
Inputs	• Process to be studied. • Related statistical performance measures. • Operational units using similar processes.
Outputs	• Statistical benchmarks of operational units. • Best practice benchmarks in organisation.
Involvement	Process owners, operational units, project manager.
Process	The project manager agrees the operational units which will be benchmarked. Process owners generate statistical benchmarks for each process. Process owner consolidates the total questionnaire for each operational unit and is careful to define each benchmark to avoid ambiguity. Operational unit managers submit their returned performance measurements to project managers.

CUSTOMER BENCHMARKING - Activity Sheet (cont'd)

ACTIVITY M1	Collect and analyse
Objective	*To combine the data gathering from process and statistical benchmarks and to draw conclusions and actionable points.*
Inputs	• *Statistical benchmark returns.* • *Process benchmark returns.* • *Comparable organisations.*
Outputs	• *What implications the benchmarks have for service strategy.* • *Implications for process improvement.* • *What measures are key to monitor factors.*
Involvement	*Project manager, process owners and sponsor.*
Process	*The results of the entire study are collectively analysed in each process category. Recommendations are made by the sponsor for the service strategy and process owners agree the implications for process improvement. Comparisons are made with best practice and the organisation's position assessed.*

CUSTOMER BENCHMARKING - Activity Sheet (cont'd)

ACTIVITY N1	Change plans
Objective	*To produce plans for process improvement and communicate to all those involved any realignment of the service proportions.*
Inputs	• *Benchmarking analysis and actions required.* • *Existing skills and competitiveness.* • *Technology constraints.*
Outputs	• *Target process definition.* • *People implications, e.g., training, recruitment, communication.* • *Target culture required.* • *Technology requirements.* • *Communication plans, internal and external.* • *Time /responsibility based plan.*
Involvement	*Project manager, benchmarking sponsor, process owner, IT managers, top management team.*
Process	*The benchmarking analysis is provided as input to the change management process. This tends to involve all process owners with the recommendations for change being made to the top management team.*

APPENDIX II:

EXAMPLE OF STATISTICAL BENCHMARKING SURVEY

UNDERSTAND CUSTOMERS

1. How do you identify who your current customers are?

- [ ] A data-base of all customers
- [ ] Current active accounts
- [ ] Written surveys
- [ ] Focus groups
- [ ] Exit interviews

2. How do you gather information about potential customers?

- [ ] Written
- [ ] Telephone surveys
- [ ] Focus groups
- [ ] Interviews
- [ ] Exit interviews
- [ ] Not applicable

3. How often do you re-examine the information you have about current and potential customers?

- [ ] Every 3 months
- [ ] Every 6 months
- [ ] Annually
- [ ] Every 2 years
- [ ] Every 3 years or longer

4. What percentage of your customers are identified?

Volume ☐ %
Depth ☐ %

5. What percentage of your overall customer/market research budget do you spend on identifying customers?

☐ %

5a. What percentage of your specific customer service budget do you spend on identifying customers?

☐ %

6. How do you identify the segments within each customer group?

☐ By location
☐ By product purchased
☐ By type of business of customer
☐ By nature of the service the customers receive
☐ By volume of transactions
☐ By value of the clients to your organisation
☐ Other (please specify)

____

____

____

☐ Not applicable

7. What percentage of your customers are clearly differentiated into segments?

☐ %

7a. What percentage of your customers represents the largest segment?

☐ %

8. Do you research:

	YES	NO
Needs		
Wants		
Expectations		
Perceptions		

LEADERSHIP THROUGH PEOPLE

1. Do you have selection criteria which specifically examine the knowledge, skills, attitudes and attributes required to perform customer service?

☐ Yes ☐ No

2. Do you use specific exercises to test if individuals can perform a service function?

☐ Yes ☐ No

3. Do you use psychological tests to look for features that relate to customer service?

☐ Yes ☐ No

3a. How much do you spend identifying training needs for customer service employees?

£ ☐

4. What percentage of frontline employees are eligible to receive some form of reward?

☐ %

5. Do you measure your culture?

☐ Yes ☐ No

5a. If yes, how do you measure this?

☐ Written survey
☐ Telephone survey
☐ Focus groups
☐ Interviews
☐ Other (please specify)

____

____

____

MANAGING DISSATISFACTION

1. What percentage of your recorded complaints are:

Written ☐ %?
Verbal ☐ %?

1a. What percentage of your complaints are:

Recorded ☐ %?
Not recorded ☐ %?

2. How do you store the information you have about complaints?

☐ Computerised system with organisation-wide access
☐ Computerised system with site-by-site access
☐ Organisation-wide manual system
☐ Manual system in each site
☐ Other (please specify)

____

____

____

3. Do you calculate the costs of losing a customer?

☐ Yes ☐ No

3a. What is the cost of losing a customer?

£ ☐

4. Do you calculate the cost of gaining a customer?

☐ Yes ☐ No

4a. What is the cost of gaining a customer?

£ ☐

5. Have you identified the areas that produce most complaints?

☐ Yes ☐ No

6. Do you have a recovery process developed for customer complaints?

☐ Yes ☐ No

6a. If you provide training, what percentage of your frontline staff have received this training?

☐ %

7. What percentage of your complaints can be resolved by frontline employees 'on-the-spot'?

☐ %

8. Do you use complaints as a source of information for improving processes?

☐ Yes ☐ No

8a. What do you do to analyse complaints?

- [ ] A special complaints task force to analyse the complaints and suggest remedial actions
- [ ] Line managers consider complaints relevant to their area of responsibility
- [ ] The Customer Service group analyses the complaints and develops action plans
- [ ] Frontline employees are asked to recommend change
- [ ] Other (please specify)

____

____

____

9. Do you tell customers what has happened as a result of their complaint?

[ ] Yes [ ] No

9a. If yes, in what percentage of cases do you notify customers?

[ ] %

10. Do you offer some form of compensation to a complaining customer (i.e., replacement service at no cost, flowers, champagne, etc)?

[ ] Yes [ ] No

10a. If yes, what percentage of customers receive this?

[ ] %

10b. If yes, how much does this cost per person?

£ [ ]

BIBLIOGRAPHY

'Anthropologists in the corporate jungle'. *Training: The Magazine of Human Resource Development,* April 1989.

'At Digital a resignation reveals key problem: selling'. *Wall Street Journal,* 27 April 1994.

'Avoiding culture conflict: dangers threaten long-term client–firm relationships'. *Public Relations Journal,* May 1991.

'Avon's strategic shift'. *Wall Street Journal.* 8–9 April 1994.

Chip Bell and Ron Zemke, *Managing Knock Your Socks Off Service.* American Management Association, 1992.

Benchmarking Best Practice, An Executive Guide. UK Department of Trade and Industry, 1993.

Tony Bendell, Louise Boulter and John Kelly, *Benchmarking for Competitive Advantage.* Financial Times/Pitmans, 1994.

John Brady and Ian Davis, 'Marketing's mid-life crisis'. *The McKinsey Quarterly,* No.2, 1993.

Business Restructuring in The Pharmaceutical Industry. Report on the proceedings. 16–17 September, IBC Technical.

'Corporate tribes'. *Business Month,* June 1989, p. 55.

'Corporate zits beware'. *Financial Times,* 14 April 1994, p. 19.

'Customer first'. *The Daily Telegraph,* 22 March 1994.

The 1993 Customer Management Forum. Report of the proceedings. Price Waterhouse, London.

'EFQM self-assessment guidelines'. The European foundation for quality management, 1994.

'The gold mine of data in customer service'. *Business Week,* 21 March 1994, pp. 40–1.

G. Hall, J. Rosenthal and J. Wade, 'How to make reengineering really work'. *Harvard Business Review,* November–December 1993.

Mack Hanan and Peter Karp, *Customer Satisfaction.* American Management Association, 1991.

Robert Heller, 'IBM's fall from grace'. *Management Journal for Quality and Service Excellence*, June 1994.

'Japanese management philosophies: from the vacuous to the brilliant'. *California Management Review,* Winter 1992.

K. Jennings and F. Westfall, 'Benchmarking for strategic action'. *Journal of Business Strategy,* May/June 1992.

Dr Milind M. Lele 'Managing Customer Satisfaction'. Seminars in Marketing Management, University of Chicago, 1994.

J. A. Schmidt, 'The link between benchmarking and shareholder value'. *Journal of Business Strategy,* May/June 1992.

'The Sunday Times customer care supplement'. *The Sunday Times*, 15 May 1994.

'Ten reasons why total quality is less than total'. *Training:* The Magazine of Human Resource Development, October 1989.

'Togo packs a continent's worth of diversity into one tiny country; its home to over 40 tribal cultures'. *Travel Weekly,* 29 January 1990.

'UPS tries to deliver more to its customers: labor problems grow'. *Wall Street Journal,* 27–28 May.

Rob Walker, *Rank Xerox-Management Revolution. Long Range Planning*, Vol. 25, No.1, pp. 9–21, Pergamon, 1992.

'Customer Intimacy'. Trecy and Wiersema, January–February 1993, Harvard Business Review Vol. 71, No.1.

INDEX

absenteeism 92
activity sheets 190–202
advertising of hotlines 130
Air France 36
American Home Products 184
analysis of performance
  process benchmarking 117–21
assets
  return on 150
AT&T 133, 159
auditing profession 38
automotive industry 8, 9, 153
  and customer satisfaction 13–15
  and telephone hotlines 125, 126, 128, 129, 130
Avis 75–6
Avon cosmetics 161–3, 164–6, 168–70

Bain management consultancy 6
banking industry 4, 37, 79, 153
Bausch & Lomb 184
Bell, Chip 46, 140
benchmarking 16–18
  against competitors 20–1, 34
  definition 20
  difficulties of 25–6, 176–7
  four steps of 19–20
  internal 23–4
  levels of 21–3, 24–5
  project plan 189
  setting up studies 176
  see also process benchmarking; statistical benchmarking; strategic benchmarking
BMW 151
body language 66
BP (British Petroleum) 5, 159
Braintree District Council 24
branding
  and customer satisfaction 11–12
Branson, Richard 79
Bristol-Myers Squibb 184
British Aerospace 151
British Petroleum (BP) 5, 159
BT 67, 133
Burmah Castrol 152–3
Burroughs Wellcome 184
business process engineering 168
  see also re-engineering

call centres 130, 131
Canon 16
capital
  cost of 150
car industry *see* automotive industry
Care 184
case studies
  Avon cosmetics 161–3, 164–6, 168–70
  multisector project 175–83
  Packaging International 81–5, 88–90, 93–4, 98–9, 102–8, 117–21
  pharmaceutical industry 183–5
change management 160–72
  assessing 171–2
  difficulties of 161–3
  evaluating position 164–6
  implementing 170–1
  processes 166–70
Chattem 184
CIBA 184
Clinton, Bill 5
Club Mediterane 20–1
Combe 184
communications
  with customers 90, 121, 127
  see also hotlines
companies
  see organisations
competencies
  benchmarking 62–9
competition 5, 10
  benchmarking against 20–1, 34
  evaluating 84
complaints

by customers 36, 37, 44, 49, 53, 56, 60
managing 77, 95–9
computers
telephone hotlines and purchases of 126, 128
conferences
sales 44, 50, 56
conjoint analysis 138
consultancies 8
corporation tax 150
cost of capital 150
costs
of new customers 7, 8, 152
Crosswell, Mike 178
CSI (Customer Surveys Inc) 103
culture
assessing 39–41
customer arrogant 34, 35–6, 41–7, 61
customer complacent 34, 37–8, 47–53, 61
customer passionate 34, 38–9, 53–51
customer contact personnel 91–4
customer focus groups 136–9
layout of 140–3
customer intimacy 33
customer retention 5–9, 11, 54–5
and operating margins 152
and service components 32
customer service 11–16
competencies 69
delivering through people 77, 90–4
difficulties of benchmarking 25–6
and levels of benchmarking 24–5
personnel 63
and product life cycles 13–15
see also service strategies
Customer Surveys Inc (CSI) 103
customers
complaints by 36, 37, 44, 49, 53, 56, 60
managing 70, 95–9
costs of acquiring 7, 8, 152
interviews with 138
measuring perceptions of 133–6
measuring satisfaction 77, 99–108
organisational attitudes to
arrogant 34, 35–6, 41–7, 61
complacent 34, 37–8, 47–53, 61
passionate 34, 38–9, 53–61
product recommendations from 8–9
relationships with 64–6, 77, 85–90
seeking views of 4
understanding needs of 77–85
data collection 129
activity sheet 207
customer focus groups 136–43
measuring customer perceptions 133–6
security of 184–5
databases 181
delivery times 13
deregulation 5, 10
Digital 90–1, 153, 154
Dominos Pizzas 21

economic growth 5, 152
EFQM (European Foundation of Quality Management) 178
electronic mail systems 90
employees
stimulating involvement 92
End-Use Marketing 88, 89
EQA (European Quality Award) vii, 75, 76–7, 78, 179
European Foundation of Quality Management (EFQM) 178
European Quality Award (EQA) vii, 75, 76–7, 78, 179
Exxon 21
Valdiz disaster 46–7

Federal Express 133
feedback 87, 92, 104–5
analysis of 136, 137
financial services industry 153
First Direct 33, 36, 153
fixed asset return 150
Ford Motors 36, 121
Freepost 127

gasoline retailing 14, 15
GATT agreements 5, 10, 18
General Electric 22
Grabiner, Mike 180
growth rates
economic 5, 152

Heller, Robert 36
Hewlett-Packard 91, 153–4
Hoover
airline ticket offer 79
hotlines 125–33
business received from 129
customer complaint 95
monitoring 131–3

product 90
promoting 130
trends in use of 127–8
types of transactions on 128–9

IBM 36, 133, 153, 154
ICL 10, 95
incentives
for attending focus groups 137–8
information
collecting 79, 82
innovation service strategy 31–2
internal benchmarking 23–4
activity sheet 196
internal focus groups 130
interviews
activity sheet 197
customer 138
telephone 134

Johnson & Johnson 47, 184

Kawasaki 23
Kuhn, Thomas 9

Land Rover 15
Lederle 184
Lele, Dr Milind 12
Leonard, Stewart 10, 58
Lexus 16
life cycles
of products 13–15
life insurance services 14, 15, 37–8
logistics support
for customer contact personnel 91

McNwil 184
mail order shopping 8, 23
Malcolm Baldridge Award vii, 57, 75, 76–7, 78, 178, 179
managers
appointing 191
Mandarin Hotel 3–4
market segmentation 79, 82, 107, 158
market surveys 50, 56
marketing 88, 89, 158
marketing departments 10
Marks & Spence33, 124
Mary Kay 164
Maytag 79
measurement
of customer perceptions 133–6
of customer satisfaction 77, 99–108
of process benchmarks 113–17
techniques 138
Mentholatum 184
Merck 184
Merrill Lynch 33
Microsoft 159
Midland Bank 121
Miles 184
Motorola 56, 135
six-sigma programme 31, 32, 38–9
multimedia 159
mystery customers 140, 144–5

NADT 58
niche service strategy 33
Northern Telecom 8

office equipment
telephone hotlines and purchases of 126, 128
Ogilvy and Mather 56, 86
oil companies 15, 33–4, 79, 159
operating margins 150, 152, 155, 156, 158
and types of markets 147
Oracle 159
organisational culture
see culture
organisational tribalism 40–1
organisations
customer arrogant 34, 35–6, 41–7, 61
customer complacent 34, 37–8, 47–53, 61
customer passionate 34, 38–9, 53–61
evaluating steps in process benchmarking 113–17
sharing best practices 176
Otis Elevators 95
overheads
reducing 6–7

packaging 12, 13
Packaging International
analysis of performance 117–21
delivering service through people 93–4
managing customer relationships 88–90
managing dissatisfaction 98–9
measuring customer satisfaction 102–8
and understanding customers 81–5
parallel learning vii, 63–8
Pepsi Co. 95

performance
  analysing 117–21
  measuring 113–17
personnel
  customer contact 63, 91–4
Pfizer 184
pharmaceutical industry 151, 152
  case study 183–5
Preston, James 161
price
  and service 157
Price Waterhouse 64–5, 66, 136, 152, 180
privatisation 5
process benchmarking 22–3, 24–5
  activity sheet 196
  analysis of performance 117–121
  cultural differences in 181
  delivering service through people 77, 90–4
  as focus of benchmarking initiative 177
  managing customer relationships 77, 85–90
  managing dissatisfaction 77, 95–9
  measurement of 113–117
  measuring customer satisfaction 77, 99–108
  and shareholder value 155–7
  understanding customer's needs 77–85
processes 166–70
  activity sheets 192–3, 195, 202
Proctor & Gamble 60, 184
productivity
  of call centres 130
products
  and customer satisfaction 11–12
  features of 80–81
  hotlines for 90
  incidence of problems and time since
    purchase 125, 126
  life cycles of 13–15
  recommendations from customers 8–9
  and service components 32
  value duration 150, 155, 159
profit margins 150, 152, 155, 156, 158
  and types of markets 159
profits
  and customer retention 6–7
project management 160
  activity sheet for appointing 191
promotion
  of emloyees 40, 42

quality management benchmarking
    framework 178
quantitative surveys 138, 145
questionnaires 185

Rank Xerox
  see Xerox
Rappaport, Professor 149
Rappaport model 150–1
re-engineering vii, 168, 169, 170
relationships
  with customers 64–6, 77, 85–90
Rhone-Poulenc Rorer 184
rites
  in organisations 40, 43–4, 49–50, 55–7, 60
rituals
  in organisations 40, 4–4, 49–50, 55–7, 60
Ritz Carlton Hotel 22, 57
Rover 10, 151, 153
rules
  in organisations 41, 46–7, 52–3, 58–61

sales
  and shareholder value 150, 155, 156
sales channels 12, 13
sales plans 44, 50, 52
sales targets 44, 49
Sandoz 184
SAS (Scandinavian Air System) 67–8
Schering-Plough 184
Schneider, Benjamin 39
scoring criteria
  for process benchmarks 115, 116
self–assessment benchmarking framework
    178
service
  and customer satisfaction 11–12, 14
  and price 157
service strategies
  demonstrating by organisations 33–4
  and statistical benchmarks 121–23
  templates for 31–3
  see also customer service
Sharrock, Peter 180
shareholder value
  activity sheet 190
  customer management and 152–3
  influences on 149
  value drivers 150–1, 158–60
    benchmarking 153–8
shareholders 5
shares
  valuing 147
Singapore Airlines 53

skills
  benchmarking 62–69
SmithKline Beecham 184
South-West Airlines 21
staff turnover 92
stakeholders
  readiness to change 165
statistical benchmarking 23, 24–5
  activity sheets 194, 198–200
  and customer service strategies 121–23
  and shareholder value 141, 143, 146, 153, 155, 158
  survey example 205–10
  uses of 123–27
Sterling Winthrop 184
strategic benchmarking 19–20, 22–3, 21–22, 24–5
  culture 34–41
  service strategies 31–4
  skills and competencies 62–9
Strategic Planning Institute 6
suggestion systems 92
Survey Research Centre 184
surveys 134, 185
  customer satisfaction 103–4
  quantitative 18, 145
  statistical benchmarking example 205–10
  telephone 82

TARP 95
tax
  corporation 150
Taylorism vii, 10
teams 84
Technical Marketing 88, 89
technology
  support for customer contact personnel 91
  used in call centres 131
telephones
  free phone numbers 90
  interviews on 134
  surveys on 82
  see also hotlines
3M Corporation 31
totems
  in organisations 40–1, 44–5, 50–2, 57–8, 61
trade agreements 5
trade shows 82
training 48–9, 55, 92
  for call centre staff 131
  for customers 15
  for senior management 64
transactional service strategy 32–3

Unilever 17
United Parcels of America 163
United Technologies 178
Upjohn 184

Valdiz disaster 46–7
voice mail systems 90

Walsh, Jack 22
Warner Lambert 184
warranties 107
Wellcome 151
white goods
  telephone hotlines and purchases of 126, 128
working capital 150

Xerox 10, 16–17, 59

Zenbara 9, 16–17
Zenke, Ron 140